# A Guide to Early Years Practice
## 2nd Edition

This timely book is a practical, accessible guide to early years practice. The author examines current theories about how children learn best and focuses on how we can support and extend the learning of young children. This fully revised and updated edition provides detailed coverage of the Foundation Stage and Early Learning Goals, including discussion of the principles underpinning these initiatives and their implications. Throughout there are case study examples to illustrate how these goals can be achieved, and advice on how to successfully involve parents as equal partners in the education of their children.

This book is essential reading for students on early years courses, and will be of interest to anyone concerned with the care and education of young children.

**Sandra Smidt** currently teaches at the University of East London. She is also the editor of *The Early Years: A Reader,* published by Routledge (1998).

# A Guide to Early Years Practice
# 2nd Edition

Sandra Smidt

RoutledgeFalmer
Taylor & Francis Group

LONDON AND NEW YORK

First published 1998
by Routledge

This edition published 2002
by RoutledgeFalmer
11 New Fetter Lane, London EC4P 4EE

Simultaneously published in the USA and Canada
by RoutledgeFalmer
29 West 35th Street, New York NY 10001

Reprinted 2003 (three times), 2004

*RoutledgeFalmer is an imprint of the Taylor & Francis Group*

© 1998, 2002 Sandra Smidt

Typeset in Garamond and Gill by BC Typesetting, Bristol
Printed and bound in Great Britain by
MPG Books Ltd, Bodmin

*British Library Cataloguing in Publication Data*
A catalogue record for this book is available from the British Library

*Library of Congress Cataloging in Publication Data*
Smidt, Sandra, 1943–
        A guide to early years practice/Sandra Smidt.–2nd ed.
           p.   cm.
        Includes bibliographical references and index.
        ISBN 0–415–26616–5
        1. Early childhood education–Great Britain. 2. Child development–
        Great Britain. I. Title.

        LB11393.3.G7 S65 2002
        372.21'0941–dc21                                   2001048686

ISBN 0–415–26616–5

# Contents

# Chapter 1

# Understanding how young children learn best

Michael Chung is four years old. He goes to playgroup four mornings a week. At home his family speak Cantonese and English and Michael is fluent in both languages. One morning Michael arrives at playgroup. He takes off his coat and hangs it on his peg. He greets all the adults and heads straight for the home corner. He selects a doll, carefully undresses the doll and then places the doll in a plastic bucket of water in order to bath her. He holds the doll in one arm whilst he pretends to squeeze shampoo from an empty bottle on the doll's head. He rubs the head gently, using one hand to shield the doll's eyes and all the time he talks to the doll in a crooning voice, saying things like, 'Don't cry. It will be all right. It will be nice and clean.' When he is satisfied that the doll is clean he lifts her out of the water, wraps her in a towel and starts to dress her. First he puts on a disposable nappy, then a vest, then a 'babygro'. That done, he picks up an empty feeding bottle and begins to feed the baby, this time singing to her. Finally, he puts the doll on his shoulder, pats her back and puts her down in a box which serves as a cot. Then he leaves the home corner, and goes over to a table where writing materials have been set out. He selects a blank booklet and begins to make marks on the pages, working from the front of the booklet to the back. Finally he takes a pencil and carefully writes his name on the front of the booklet and places it in the pocket of his coat to take home.

An everyday event in any playgroup, nursery or group. Nothing that Michael did was remarkable or surprising and most people observing Michael would have said that he was playing in the way most young children play. But this little vignette tells us quite a lot about Michael and gives us an insight into what he already knows, what he can do, what he is interested in and how he chooses to spend his time. Information like this is essential to anyone working with young children.

In this opening chapter we will look at what is currently known about how young children learn – and, most crucially, we will examine theories about how young children learn best. We do know that young children can be taught to do many things in many different ways. Our concern is to examine the best ways to promote learning in young children.

## What we mean by learning

'Learning' is a word we all use frequently and often without really considering what it means. It is a word we use to describe an enormous range of experiences and events. To illustrate this, consider these statements:

> 'I learned early on, that I wanted to be famous.'
> 'Children learn through play.'
> 'When I first learned to read I couldn't get enough books.'
> 'Jamie learned to talk at nine months.'
> 'I learned to drive.'
> 'At school I had to learn poetry off by heart.'
> 'I never learned another language.'
> 'I used to hate olives, but then I learned to love them.'

If you analyse each of these you will find that we sometimes use the word learning to talk about how we acquire skills – learning to drive, to walk or to use a knife and fork, for example. We use the word to talk about how we acquire attitudes – learning to enjoy the books or appreciate the taste of olives. We use the word to describe how we appreciate how to relate to other people. In short, the word 'learning' is a broad term that defines what happens to us in a range of circumstances and over an indefinite period of time. You will know that children learn at home, in the playground, at school, in the streets. Learning happens all the time.

What is actually happening when we learn is that connections between cells in the brain are laid down and strengthened. So 'learning' also has a very precise meaning. At birth, the human infant has all the brain cells needed for human development. In order for the human being to function, however, connections or pathways need to be formed between these cells. You will have read that learning during the first five years of life is more rapid than at any other time. This is why the early years of life are so crucial in terms of learning. You will find more about brain research towards the end of this chapter.

Let us pause at this point and return to the case study of Michael, which opened this chapter.

*Write down all the things you have learned in the past four years. Now write down all the things that Michael has learned in the past four years.*

Your list might have included things like:

- learned to make meringues
- learned to use an electric drill
- learned to tango

In the list of what Michael has learned you might have included things like:

- learned to sit
- learned to stand
- learned to walk
- learned to use both hands in conjunction
- learned to understand and speak two languages
- learned how to bath a baby
- learned how to use a pencil
- learned how to behave at playgroup

You will realise from this just how accelerated learning is in the first few years of life. As we get older we do continue learning, but the rate decreases dramatically.

So we have established that learning means something very precise in terms of what happens physiologically. Many researchers and theorists have studied the development of children and their work is useful to those of us working with young children as it gives us a framework in which to plan our work. It also helps us to justify what we do to parents and to other practitioners. We will start by looking at some of the things the most influential theorists have to say and later in this book we will refer to them to support what we are saying.

## The work of Jean Piaget

We will start by looking at the work of Jean Piaget, a Swiss theorist who studied his own children and children in groups. His work is important for a number of reasons. In the first place, he was the first person to show that the human infant is not passive, but actively tries to get meaning from all the experiences he or she encounters. Prior to this, people had believed that the infant had to be 'fed' experiences, but Piaget showed that the human infant is an 'active learner'. Many people, when they first encounter this idea, think it refers to the fact that the infant is physically active and learns through this. Piaget meant, however, that the human infant is mentally or cognitively active. In other words, the human infant is busy trying to understand the world and each experience results in changes in mental function.

To explain this Piaget used the terms 'accommodation' and 'assimilation'. Assimilation is seen as the process of taking in new information, of adding to the existing experiences and sometimes changing these. Remember that all of this happens in the brain. Accommodation is the next stage of learning and is when the child or infant uses information in the brain in order to adapt to the environment. You will realise from this that Piaget saw accommodation as the higher-order cognitive process, the one that allows us to solve problems.

The second reason for looking at the work of Piaget is that his work has had a profound effect on the school system in England. In his work he speculated that all children passed through clearly defined stages of development. The first stage, which he called the Sensori-motor stage, lasted from birth to the age of two. The second stage – which he called the stage of Pre-operational Thought – lasted from two to about seven. The stage of Operational Thought followed and was thought to continue to the age of about eleven. The final stage, that of Formal Operations, continued into adulthood. You will realise that these stages correspond closely with the English schools system: nursery/ infant from three to seven; junior from eight to eleven; secondary from eleven to adulthood.

Now it is important to note that, although Piaget's work was very important and influential, much of it has been criticised and the largest body of criticism relates to this stage theory of development. At first glance you may think that what you have read so far makes sense. To anyone involved with children it is clear that children do develop and that the behaviour and learning of a seven-year-old is very different from that of a three-year-old. Piaget, however, tended to focus on what children could not yet do rather than looking at what they could do.

Let us take an example and analyse it to see what it tells us about what the child can do and about what the child cannot do yet.

> Four-year-old Rehana paints a picture at the easel, takes a pencil and makes some marks in the top right hand corner of the page. The first mark is clearly an attempt at the 'R' with which her name begins.

If you were considering what she knows you might say that she knows that she ought to write her name on her painting and that she knows the first letter of her name. If you were considering what she doesn't yet know you might say that she doesn't yet know how to write her name properly. For those of us working with children it is much more important to know what children already know and can do. This allows us to plan what to offer the child next in order to help them take the next step in learning.

In devising the stages Piaget tended to focus on what children could not yet do. This is particularly true of children in the Pre-operational stage, which is the stage which most concerns us. According to Piaget children under the age of about seven are not able to think logically or to conserve ideas of number, length, capacity or volume. Piaget's theories about this stage came from a number of experiments he did with children where he gave them tasks to do. Many of these are well known, as, for example, giving children two identical lumps of plasticine and then dividing one lump into a number of smaller lumps. The child was then asked, 'Are they the same?' Younger children tended to answer that they were not the same, that the lump that had been divided up into several smaller lumps 'had more'. Some critics of Piaget point out that since the children had witnessed the adult dividing up one lump of plasticine, they must have assumed that this had to be a trick question. Other critics suggest that the children couldn't see the point of the activity or of the question and so tended to give the answer they thought the adult wanted to hear.

Piaget also said that young children in the Pre-operational stage are not able to take on the perspective of someone else. In other words, young children are what he called 'egocentric': they see themselves as being central to everything and cannot see the world from anyone else's point of view. He did not mean that young children are selfish, but that they cannot mentally put themselves into the position of someone else. To illustrate this he carried out an experiment involving three papier mâché mountains. The young child was placed in front of these models and then a doll was put in a position offering a different view of the mountains. The children were asked to select the drawing which showed the view the doll could see. Very few of these young children were able to do this; they tended to select the picture showing the view they could see. For Piaget this was evidence enough.

*How do you feel about this? Have you encountered young children who are able to demonstrate that they are able to appreciate what it feels like to be in someone else's shoes? How about the child who rushes over to comfort a friend who has fallen and grazed her knee?*

James McGarrigle (cited in Donaldson 1978) tried a different experiment to demonstrate that young children are able to take on the view of someone else. Children were told that a teddy had been naughty and were then asked to hide the teddy from a policeman doll. Many of the young children were able to do this. The reasons for this are both interesting and directly relevant to our work with young children. McGarrigle believed that these young children were able to 'decentre' (that is, to take on the views of another) when what they were asked to do made sense to them. He also believed that young children demonstrate what they know best when they are able to draw on their previous experience. In his 'Naughty Teddy' experiment he felt that many of the young children had had experience of hiding things or of hiding themselves. They also might have had experience of being 'naughty' and could see why the teddy might need to be hidden from the policeman.

A pause now, to draw breath and to pull out the two main themes of this section:

- From birth, human infants actively seek to understand their world.
- Young children learn best when they can see the purpose of what they are doing and when they are able to draw on their previous experience.

## The work of Margaret Donaldson

Let us now turn to the work of a more recent theorist, Margaret Donaldson. She was one of Piaget's fiercest critics and the person who motivated McGarrigle in much of his research. In her book *Children's Minds*, published in 1978, she looked at how children are taught when they first start school and related it to what was known about how young children learn. The learning children are required to do when they start formal schooling is what Donaldson called 'decontextualised', which means that it is not rooted in a context. Take, for example, children being asked to colour in a set of balloons on a worksheet. This is not something that is set in a context that makes sense to young children. Why are they being asked to do this? What purpose does it serve? Will it matter if the big balloon is red rather than blue? As a contrast you might like to consider the young child painting spontaneously at an easel and selecting which colours to use.

Abstract learning – which describes much of the learning children do at school – is very difficult for young learners. They need to be able to draw on their previous experience and to use practical tools and activities to help them make sense of what they are doing. Of course, all children do need to be able to cope with abstract learning. We would not expect children to go through life always needing physical props and lifelike activities in order to learn. The crucial point Donaldson makes is that children need to be led gradually and gently into abstract learning and that this will happen best if children are allowed a range of experiences in settings which are familiar and which make 'human sense' to them. Donaldson calls settings like these 'meaningful contexts'.

To illustrate this more clearly let us examine some familiar activities which can be described as meaningful contexts:

> The children in the playgroup are baking cookies with an adult. They have been to the shops in order to buy the ingredients and one child handed over the money to the shopkeeper and got the change. The adult had a shopping list and had told the children what ingredients they would need. Back in the playgroup each child has a mixing bowl and each is involved in beating together the ingredients, sifting the flour and spooning the mixture into cookie tins.

*Can you see how this might be described as a 'meaningful context'?*

All children will have had experience of going to the shops. They know that you need to buy things and that that involves some exchange of money. They have probably been to the shops with someone carrying a shopping list. Moreover, all children are familiar with food, with cooking and with eating. So it is an activity whose purpose is clear (delicious cookies to eat!) and one which is familiar.

> The staff in the nursery have set up a baby clinic in a corner of the room. Two children have recently had baby sisters. The clinic is equipped with some posters and leaflets obtained from the local baby clinic up the road, weighing scales, a baby bath, some dolls, some clipboards, a stethoscope donated by a parent and a doll's cot.

*Can you see how this might be described as a 'meaningful context'?*

Here again, many children will have had some experience of going to a clinic and those with younger siblings may have accompanied parents to the baby clinic.

It is easy to see how activities like this are both familiar and meaningful to children. What many people find difficult to understand (and sometimes to explain to parents) is what children are actually learning as they play in settings like these. In order to answer this question we need to look more closely at what we mean by 'play'. Everyone working with young children knows that play is important. We often say things like 'Children learn through play' or 'Play is children's work'. But what do we mean by play and how can we be sure that play is so important in the early years?

## The importance of play

Many researchers and theorists have written about play. You may be familiar with the books by Tina Bruce or Janet Moyles. What is special about play is that it is something the child has chosen to do. So if you tell a child to go and play with the Lego, for example, the child has not chosen to do this and what the child does cannot properly be described as play. When a child has chosen to do something this indicates that the child is following some interest of his or her own. The child is then free to follow this interest and pursue it, often over a long period of time. Here is an example:

> Hannah is thirteen months old. She is playing outdoors with a plastic bowl of water, a paintbrush, a scrubbing brush, a sieve and a small container. The adults with her have shown her how to paint with water on the yard floor. Because, like most children, she is obliging she copies what the adults do for a few seconds. But her real interest lies elsewhere. She scuttles backwards and forwards between her mother and the plastic bowl, carrying both brushes in one hand. She hands the brushes to her mother, takes them back, returns to the bowl,

places them in the water, takes them out, returns to her mother and so on. The activity lasts for more than forty minutes.

It is difficult to know what Hannah is doing as she plays. Perhaps she is exploring the distance between the bowl and her mother. Perhaps she is perfecting her newly developed skill of holding two objects in one hand. But what is clear is that this is something in which she is deeply engrossed and that she pursues for a long period of time. We often hear people say that young children have a 'limited concentration span'. This is only true when children are doing things they have been told to do rather than things they have chosen to do.

Because children have chosen what they do when they play, they set their own goals. The second important feature of play is that it carries no risk of failure. The child has decided what to do and therefore cannot fail. No one has set the child goals that are too difficult or even too easy. The purpose of the play is in the child's hands.

A theorist who wrote a great deal about play was the Russian psychologist Vygotsky. He was particularly interested in two aspects of play. Firstly he believed that in play, particularly in imaginative play, children operate at their highest level of intellectual functioning, way beyond their everyday competence. He believed that, in play, a child stands 'a head taller' than him- or herself. What he meant by this was that when you observe children engaged in imaginative play and pay close attention to what they are doing, they demonstrate knowledge and abilities that you would not see when the children are in a different situation. Here is an example to illustrate this:

> Johan is in the reception class. He finds it difficult to do the tasks expected of him — writing, doing number work, colouring in and so on. But his teacher was surprised to notice that when he was out in the playground playing 'pirates' on the climbing frame he was able to express ideas, solve problems, communicate his thoughts and ideas and negotiate with the other children. In his imaginative play he stood a 'head taller' than he appeared in the classroom.

The second aspect of play that interested Vygotsky was how, through play, children begin to understand what is called 'the symbolic function'. A symbol is something that stands for or represents something else. Our spoken language is symbolic. The word 'dog' stands for or represents the living creature. Our written language is symbolic. The letters 'd-o-g' stand for that same living creature. Our number system is symbolic. The symbol '2' means more than one and less than three. In order to live in the real world all children need to come to understand how one thing can stand for another.

In imaginative play children, from very early on, begin to use one thing to represent another. The young child who places a block to her ear and pretends it is a telephone is doing just this. This experience of making one thing stand for another is a vital part of learning since many of the ways in which we describe and represent the world are symbolic. You have only to look around you and observe the written words, hear the sounds, notice the logos and pictures and numerals to realise how important this is. In order to learn to read and write, to talk, to build and draw, to count and measure and to communicate your thoughts and ideas, this knowledge is vital.

Another pause and time to draw out the main themes from these two sections:

- Abstract learning is difficult for young children who need a lot of experience of doing things, handling objects, and exploring the physical and social world.
- Children learn best in situations which make 'human sense' to them.
- Children learn best when they have chosen what to do – i.e. when they play.
- Through play children demonstrate all that they know. Observing children at play and paying close attention to what they are actually doing is our best way of understanding what they already know and are interested in.
- Through imaginative play children begin to understand how to use one thing to represent another – an essential skill in learning how to describe and communicate thoughts and ideas.

## The role of adults

So far we have looked at what the children are doing and not made much mention of what the adults involved with young children do to support and extend their learning. Piaget believed that all that the adults working with young children needed to do was to provide them with an interesting and stimulating environment. This is important, of course. Children do need to encounter new and exciting activities and objects to explore. But some theorists have paid more attention to the role of adults and it is to their work we turn now.

Vygotsky was not only interested in play. Like Piaget, he saw the child as an active learner, but for him the context in which learning took place was vital. He was interested in how knowledge is passed on from one generation to another and, by definition, this implies that people around the child have an important role to play. Vygotsky viewed learning as an essentially social activity. Piaget was more interested in how children acquire knowledge and his view is thus more focused on the individual child than on the child in society.

Vygotsky believed that children are able to perform at a higher level when they are offered help than if left to struggle on their own. He called the gap between what a child could do unaided and what the child could do with help the 'Zone of Proximal Development'. It is important to understand that this is not something visible to the naked eye. It represents the child's potential. Perhaps an example will make this clear:

Dana is pretending to write in the writing area of her nursery (Figure 1.1). The nursery nurse watching her notices that in her pretend writing are some letter shapes, including the D and the A from her name. The adult comments on the fact that Dana already knows how to write some of the letters in her name.

Figure 1.1 Dana's first attempt at writing her name. You can see that the 'D' and 'A' are included in her string of letter-like shapes.

The next time Dana pretends to write (Figure 1.2) she again makes lots of marks and some letter-like shapes, but this time she says she is writing her name as she writes the D, the A and the N of her name.

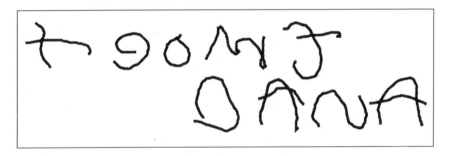

Figure 1.2 Dana's second attempt at writing her name. This time you can see that, whilst she still includes a string of letter-like shapes, she has managed to write her name separately.

The adult, by paying careful attention to what Dana was doing, has helped Dana to develop from including some of the letters she knows from her name to writing her name recognisably. The adult has helped the child perform at a higher level, thus bridging the Zone of Proximal Development.

Jerome Bruner, another theorist who has studied the development of young children, describes what the adult has done in the above example as 'scaffolding' the child's learning. A scaffold is something that is erected to help builders gradually construct a building. Once the building is in place the scaffold is removed. Bruner believed that adults can allow children to take small, supported steps in their learning. When the learning is complete, the support of the adult is no longer needed.

In order successfully to scaffold learning the adult has to understand both what the child already knows and what the child is paying attention to. The worker in the above example guessed that Dana was interested in writing the letters of her own name. In this case she was right, but there is no guarantee. One way in which you know that you have been correct in your guess is by the child's response. Children quickly let you know when you are way off-beam!

Here is an example to show what happens when the adult follows his or her own agenda rather than successfully tuning in to what the child is paying attention to:

> Harinder, playing in the home corner, brings the playgroup worker a plastic plate on which she has placed some wooden blocks, some bits of plasticine and some beads. 'It's dinner,' she announces, 'sausages and beans and chips.'
>
> 'Oh, thank you!' replies the worker. 'How many sausages have you got? Can you count them?'
>
> Harinder picks up the plate and moves away.

The worker saw the opportunity to assess the child's knowledge of counting. But counting the sausages was not what Harinder was interested in. Her response was to walk away from the adult. Instead of her learning having been taken forward it was effectively stopped.

So it is important to try and understand the child's purposes. It is also important to start with what the child already knows. Scaffolding sometimes involves breaking down the task into smaller tasks; sometimes helping the child to become aware of what he or she has achieved; sometimes helping the child sequence what he or she is doing and sometimes helping the child focus on an aspect of the task which is relevant. These are things that many parents and practitioners do almost instinctively.

Scaffolding learning is a skill well worth developing. Here are some examples of adults scaffolding learning:

> Joshua (aged eleven months) puts his empty bottle against the doll's face. His mother says, 'Oh Josh! You are feeding the doll'.

> Malindi (aged four years, two months) is retelling the story of 'We're going on a Bear Hunt' from the book and, by mistake, turns over two

pages. The nursery worker comments on this and helps her find the right page, so that her retelling of the story continues in the correct order.

Manna (aged four years, seven months) is working with junk materials and announces that she is making a microwave for her mother. She has gathered together a large number of boxes and containers and seems to have lost her way. The teacher suggests she starts off by selecting one box for the microwave. Once that is done she guides Manna in selecting the other materials she will need to complete her chosen task.

It should be clear from this that both Bruner and Vygotsky saw the role of adults as crucial. They saw the interaction between the child and adult as one of the most important features of any learning that takes place. When the adult intervenes in the learning situation, the interaction must be sensitive and the adult should not attempt to test the child or to stretch the child too far. To illustrate this, here are some examples. You might like to assess them to see if you feel that the adult's intervention fulfils the criteria laid out above:

Louisa is nearly six. She has been working on making a boat out of junk materials. She has been experiencing difficulty in getting the materials to stick together.
'Oh I need some more glue,' she said and put more glue on and held it tight. 'If it doesn't work this time I'm not going to use it.' As she let go of it, it fell off. She took it and threw it across the table in anger.
'What about using an elastic band?' I suggested. Louisa agreed and held the form in place while I put an elastic band over it.
'Good, it worked!' she said, looking at the other children. 'That's good, isn't it, using an elastic band?'

(Bragg 1998, pp. 144–5)

Two four-year-olds, Damian and Willy, are playing with magnets.
Damian puts the magnets on the table. They attract. He then picks up one of the magnets and a wooden brick. Nothing happens. He tries with the glue pot. Again, nothing happens.
'It won't stick to the brick or the glass, but it sticks to the paper clip,' I said and then added 'I wonder why?'
Damian tries the sponge and then the metal sharpener. As the sharpener moves across the table towards the magnet Damian begins to laugh.
'That shoots down, look!'
He picks up the spoon.
'Yeah, a spoon'll stick and a knife. Both do stick to the magnet. It's a bit of a funny trick.'
I then said, 'Some things did stick, but some didn't.'

Later the boys are joined by three-year-old Ollie who asks, 'Do hands stick?'

He picks up one of the magnets and holds it against the palm of his hand.

Damian responds, 'No.'

'Why?' asks Ollie.

'Because it hasn't got the thing – the magnet thing.'

I repeat his response, 'The magnet thing?'

Damian goes on 'The bit that sticks.'

(Lanigan 1998, p. 35)

You will have realised that in each example 'I' referred to the adult. You will also notice, in the second example, how the children were learning from one another. Vygotsky emphasised that children learn from one another and that more advanced children often provide models for younger children.

Let us now summarise the key points from this section:

- Adults have a key role to play in providing an environment which is stimulating and challenging.
- Adults need to understand what children already know and can do in order to help children develop and learn.
- Adults need to pay careful attention to what children are interested in or are paying attention to.
- Adults need to ensure that their intervention is sensitive and focused on the child's interests and not on their own agenda.
- Scaffolding children's learning helps children bridge the gap between what they can do alone and what they can do with help.

## The importance of language in learning

You will remember that Piaget believed that the role of the adult was primarily to provide a stimulating and challenging environment in which children could learn. He saw language as a system of symbols for representing the world and as something quite separate from the actions which led to reasoning and the development of logical thinking. He believed that explaining things to small children, before they were 'ready' was a waste of time. Using words to help children make sense of situations led to children learning what have been called 'empty procedures'. This view of the adult use of language is held by certain practitioners today who believe in what is called 'heuristic play'. Young children are invited to explore new and interesting objects physically without the verbal intervention of adults. Supporters of this approach believe that this allows children to become deeply immersed in what they are doing and prevents them from being distracted by the adult intervention.

Vygotsky and Bruner, by contrast, both regard language as essential to learning. Much of Bruner's early research related to how adults help children acquire language. For him language involves much more than just talk. It includes gesture, inflection, intonation, body language and signs. Through the early turn-taking games that most primary caregivers play with their infants (things like 'Peekaboo') young children begin to use language both to communicate and to understand how language itself works. Young children begin to play with language just as they play with objects in the physical world. This verbal play, according to Bruner, is an essential component of development. You will have gathered already that Bruner also believed that adults, when scaffolding learning, use language to help the child make sense of the situation, to reflect on what they already know and can do and to take the next cognitive step.

Vygotsky paid particular attention to the development of speech and thought. He believed that these have different roots but later come together so that it is almost impossible to separate them out. Can you think without language? Can you talk without thinking?

*In responding to this question you might want to consider some of the work quoted by Steven Pinker (1994) where he talks about Karen Wynn's findings that five-month-old babies, who have no words so cannot speak, can do a simple form of mental arithmetic. Does this seem like thinking to you?*

For young children speech is used at first to communicate, to make and share meanings. Later it becomes a tool of thought. By this he meant that language itself can change the way in which children think and learn.

In the earliest stages of speech Vygotsky believed that children go through a phase of talking aloud to themselves, explaining and describing what they are doing. This 'inner speech' serves to help children plan, control, recall and predict. You may have encountered young children's monologues and wondered what they were doing and why. As children get older this 'inner speech' becomes more abbreviated. Children no longer have to describe to themselves every step of what they are doing. The 'inner speech' becomes internalised as children become aware of what they are thinking. Children need to be aware of what they are thinking in order to learn.

This self-awareness comes partly through the internalisation of inner speech, but also through interactions with others. Adults often reflect back to children what they have said or done and in doing this they help children become aware of their own achievements. You can find evidence of this in the magnets example in the previous section. Where the adult draws the child's attention to something the child has done, the adult helps fill the gap between what the child can do alone and what the child can do with help – the Zone of Proximal Development. In other words, the adult allows the child to make conscious what he or she already knows and can do.

So children need both 'inner speech' and social speech (talking to and with others). Vygotsky believed that children learn first by trying to discover what something is or what it does through observing an experienced learner and learning from that. Then the child tries unaided, using 'inner speech' to explain the process. Learning is consolidated when the child internalises the concept.

Children encounter spoken language in all the activities they engage in at home. This applies to all children, whatever their backgrounds, cultures or languages. Parents, other family members, friends and carers use language as a normal part of everyday life. Every situation you can think of is bathed in language – cooking the supper, going to the bus, walking to the shops, digging in the garden and so on. Parents know what their children are interested in and they know what their children already know and what they can do and so they are tuned into their children's needs, interests and desires. The language within the home becomes a genuine dialogue with the parent sometimes listening to the child and the child sometimes listening to the parent.

In 1984 Tizard and Hughes studied the language used by the parents of young children and contrasted it with the language used by teachers once children started at school or nursery. There had previously been the notion that working-class parents tended to use an inferior form of language at home with their children, a form of language that did not allow the children to predict, to solve problems and to move away from the here and now in their thinking. The work of Tizard and Hughes (and a subsequent study by Gordon Wells [1986]) disproved this and showed that all parents, whatever their socio-economic level, use language in order to make and share meaning and they thus enable their children to acquire language which allows them to think, to learn, to talk and to solve problems.

The failure of many poorer children in the school system cannot then be blamed on the language used within the home. What Tizard and Hughes found was that once children started school or nursery the language used by the adults was very different. Instead of engaging in genuine dialogue around lifelike problems and situations, adults in schools tended to subtly test children, often trying to get the child to give the correct answer to questions.

Let us look at two examples, one set in a home and the other in a nursery class. As you read through them try and see how the language used by the adult either helps the child by scaffolding learning or inhibits learning by refusing to pay proper attention to the child's interests.

At home three-year-old Mpo is waiting for her tea with her sister Zinzi. Their mother slices and butters bread and spreads Marmite on it.

'Here, girls,' she says as she brings the sandwiches to the table. 'I've cut each slice in half so you can have two each.'

'Two for me and two for you,' says Mpo.

'That's four,' says five-year-old Zinzi.

At nursery Mpo takes a piece of cardboard over to the teacher.

'Can you cut it in half for me?' she asks. 'The scissors are too hard for me.'

The teacher obliges and handing the two pieces of card back to the child asks, 'And what have you got?'

Mpo looks baffled. The teacher repeats the question.

'Two?' suggests Mpo hopefully.

'Two what?' persists the teacher, determined that the child use the word 'half' in her response.

'Two . . . cards.'

You will notice that in the second example the child actually requests that the adult cut the card in half. Had the adult been paying proper attention to the child she would not have had to test the child as she did.

In this section, the key points are as follows:

- Language is vital for learning, although there may well be times when children are so deeply involved in what they are doing that the adult does not need to intervene verbally.
- Children learn from watching experienced learners, by using 'inner speech' and by internalising the concept.
- Children need both 'inner speech' and social speech.
- Language which involves a genuine dialogue and allows the child to be an equal participant is more likely to take learning forward than instructing, questioning and testing.

## So what should young children be doing?

We will now turn to the work of someone writing today. Lilian Katz has spent many years considering how young children learn best. She believes that we already know a great deal about how children learn and develop and that this knowledge should inform the curriculum we offer to young children. In her paper, called 'What Should Young Children Be Learning?' (1988) she draws a distinction between what children can do and what children should do. She says:

> Just because children can do something when they are young does not mean that they should do it . . . You can make children work for gold stars and tokens and all sorts of rewards, but that doesn't mean you should. What's interesting is that almost anything you get young children to do they appear to be willing to do. They don't appear to be suffering and some of them even look as though they love it.
>
> (Katz 1988, p. 29)

For Katz, the developmental question is not just how do children learn – because children always learn. Some children learn to lie, some to cheat, some to steal, some to read. The essential question is: what is it that young children should be doing that will *best* serve their development in the long run?

Katz is not alone in believing that this is a crucial question facing educators and carers alike. Learning is about more than acquiring skills and knowledge: it involves both feelings and attitudes or what Katz calls 'dispositions'. A disposition can be defined as a habit of mind. You may have the disposition to be friendly or the disposition to be unfriendly. Almost all young children have the disposition to be curious. We have seen how children actively seek to make sense of the world and eagerly explore all new opportunities and experiences. Where children encounter inappropriate learning experiences there is a very real danger that this disposition – to be a learner – will be damaged.

*At this point you might like to pause and consider what you think might be inappropriate learning experiences for young children.*

What did you come up with? Theorists like Katz and David Elkind believe that where children encounter formal learning at too young an age they may learn the skills and knowledge required at that point, but their dispositions to be learners may be damaged. Elkind believes that children forced into formal learning too soon become less independent thinkers and tend to become very reliant on adults. They don't develop their abilities to be reflective learners or to be aware of what they can do and what they know. They are dependent on the adults around them to reward their efforts with praise, or gold stars or whatever system of approval operates in their playgroup or nursery. Such children may lose interest in what it is they are doing (the process) because all the approval they get relates to the end-product. They become like little workers on an assembly line, getting through their 'work' as quickly as possible so that they can then go on and do what really matters to them – that is, play. Children in such formal and inappropriate learning situations will not get deeply involved in what they are doing.

To summarise this section:

- Learning involves more than acquiring skills and knowledge: it also involves feelings and dispositions.
- What children do affects how they feel about themselves as learners.
- A too formal curriculum introduced at too early an age may result in children showing short-term gains in skills and knowledge, but long-term damage to their dispositions to be learners.
- Those working with young children should enable children to get deeply involved in what they are doing and, in interacting with children, should try to concentrate on what the children are doing rather than on any end-product.

## Brain studies

In recent years there has been a lot of interest in studies of what takes place in the human brain during the early years. In fact there has been so much written about the findings that massive government-funded projects have been launched in response to them. Here are two examples:

- the World Bank has started to fund programmes in countries like Uganda and the Philippines on the grounds that investment in the early years will bring about long-term gains in terms of later success in life, citing the brain research as a crucial part of the evidence;
- the Sure Start programmes in England, focused on the poorest young children and their families, adopt a model of early intervention also influenced by the brain research findings.

In view of this you might want to know some facts about the human brain in order to be able to critically evaluate some of the claims that are currently being made.

Interest in brain development has come about because of advances in technology which enable researchers to use non-invasive techniques for looking at what is going on inside the brain. The brain is an extremely complex organ and is greedy for oxygen. (This is something you might want to remember when you consider how much access the children you work with have to fresh air and exercise.)

The cerebral cortex is the area of the brain most associated with thinking and reason. It is divided into two hemispheres which are connected to one another. There is an ongoing debate about the functions of the hemispheres. Each half of the cerebrum is divided into four lobes and each of these is associated with particular activities. At the back of the brain is the occipital lobe which is primarily concerned with vision: above this is the parietal lobe which deals mainly with movement, number and orientation. The temporal lobes are associated with several activities, but chiefly with hearing and language and the frontal lobes deal with feelings, emotions, planning and decision-making amongst other higher cognitive functions.

The brain is made up of neurones which can be regarded as the building-blocks of the brain. These are so numerous that they have been compared to the number of stars in the galaxy. They are serviced, supported and repaired by even more glial cells which form a sort of 'glue'. Neurones work by forming connections or networks. They do this by sending tiny electrical signals along the axon (which is like the 'body' of the neurone) to be received by the dendrites (like the 'arms' of another neurone). It is the laying-down of connections between neurones that constitutes learning.

The brain at birth is different from the adult brain. Some connections present in infancy die out. Others have not yet been established. The lobes are not fully developed: the frontal lobe, for example, is not fully formed until young adulthood.

Those are the facts. Now let us look at what the research tells us – but do remember that the research is in its infancy and nothing is certain.

- It is a fact that the connections or synapses between neurones are laid down very rapidly in the first few years of life. In humans, by the age of about three or four, the number of these synapses has peaked and in puberty they start to reduce. Some theorists have suggested that this means that children learn most in the early years. We all know that from the earliest days the human infant is actively seeking to make sense of the world and that this seems to run parallel with the laying down of neural connections. Critics of this approach point out that there is no evidence to show that the more synapses we have the cleverer we are: we do, after all, continue to learn throughout our lives.

- Much of the research has focused on critical periods supporting the idea that if something has not developed by a particular point in time it will not develop fully. Think about how difficult it is for adults to learn a new language – something toddlers do without any apparent effort. You may have read about children who, for one reason or another, are deprived of stimulation in the early years and who then struggle to make up for this – sometimes never succeeding. Pinker(1994) says:

  > acquisition of normal language is guaranteed for children up to the age of six, is steadily compromised from then until shortly after puberty, and is rare thereafter. Maturational changes in the brain, such as the decline in metabolic rate and number of neurones during the early school-age years, and the bottoming out of the number of synapses and metabolic rate around puberty are possible causes.
  >
  > (1994, p. 319)

- The most influential body of research has looked at what are called 'enriched environments'. Much of the neuroscientific research has looked at rats and monkeys in complex environments and some of this research has shown that the brain remains plastic or flexible enough to lay down a significant number of new synapses in adulthood in response to new experiences. This may account for our ability to continue learning throughout our lives. Supporters of brain research have argued that young children need to be in enriched environments and often this term is used to mean middle-class environments full of piano lessons, classical music, educational games, etc. We all want our young children to have access to as wide a range of experiences as possible, but it is essential to remember that a rich environment does not, necessarily, mean a middle-class environment. Children living in deep poverty in Africa nonetheless learn as they experience playing in the sand with sticks and stones, working alongside adults, singing songs and hearing traditional tales, inventing games and observing the changing sky.

To summarise this section:

- New technologies are helping us discover much about how the human brain works and to use this to influence our work with young children and families.
- It is evident that children need to have many varied opportunities to learn and play.
- Care needs to be taken to ensure that we understand that an 'enriched' environment is any environment in which children can have first-hand experience, play and learn.

## A last word

In this introductory chapter we have looked briefly at what some of the theorists and researchers have said about how young children learn best. We have established that learning has a precise meaning – the establishment of connections between brain cells – and that this happens most efficiently where children are able to explore their world in as many ways as possible. Children are naturally curious and when they are encouraged to follow their own interests – that is, to play – they will become deeply involved and may spend a long time exploring something. This in-depth play is what educators are seeking to encourage in the early years.

We have explored the role of adults and seen that it involves not only providing a stimulating and challenging environment, but also interacting sensitively and in a way which is likely to help the child take the next step in learning and development. Interaction will be most supportive where the adult is able to tune in to what it is the child is interested in and in what the child is exploring. We have seen how important the role of language is in learning and how adults can use language to extend learning where they engage in genuine dialogue with children.

We have recognised that young children are very busy trying to make sense of their world. They learn by drawing on what they already know and have experienced, and need many experiences set in familiar and meaningful contexts to help them. In this way they are able to move towards being able to hold images and ideas in their heads and then to cope with the abstract learning that is required of them at school.

Many people believe that the younger you start teaching a child, the better the results will be. You will have encountered parents who eagerly teach their very young children to read and write. As Lilian Katz reminds us, young children are very obliging and will learn anything we teach them. But the consequences of such early formal learning may be negative in the long term. It is important to keep reminding ourselves that children in Britain start formal schooling at an earlier age than in any other developed country. The introduction of the Foundation Stage for children under the age of six offers us the opportunity to ensure that our young children are taught according to the important and undisputed findings cited in this chapter. Only then can we trust that they will go on to be successful learners.

## References

Bragg, S. (1998) 'Talk and Technology', in S. Smidt (ed.), *The Early Years: A Reader*, London, Routledge.

Bruce, T. (1987) *Early Childhood Education*, London, Hodder and Stoughton.

Donaldson, M. (1978) *Children's Minds*, London, Fontana.

Elkind, D. (1986) 'Formal Education and Early Childhood Education: An Essential Difference', *Phi Delta Kappa*, May.

Katz, L. (1988) 'What Should Young Children Be Learning?', *American Educator*, Summer.

Lanigan, G. (1998) 'Children Playing with Magnets', in S. Smidt (ed.), *The Early Years: A Reader*, London, Routledge.

Moyles, J. (1989) *Just Playing*, Oxford, Oxford University Press.

Moyles, J. (1998) 'To Play or Not to Play? That is the Question', in S. Smidt (ed.), *The Early Years: A Reader*, London, Routledge.

Nash, M. (1997) *Fertile Minds*, London, PCP.

Pinker, S. (1994) *The Language Instinct*, Harmondsworth, Penguin.

Smidt, S. (ed.) (1998) *The Early Years: A Reader*, London, Routledge.

Sutherland, P. (1992) *Cognitive Development Today: Piaget and his Critics*, London, PCP.

Tizard, B. and Hughes, M. (1984) *Young Children Learning: Talking and Thinking at Home and at School*, London, Fontana.

Wells, G. (1987) *The Meaning Makers: Children Learning Language and Using Language to Learn*, London, Hodder and Stoughton.

# Chapter 2

# How to support and extend the learning of young children

In the first chapter we examined some of the theories and research concerning how young children learn best. We touched on the role of the adult and, in this chapter, we will go into this in more detail. For those of us working with young children a sound understanding of how children learn is only of use to us if we are able to act on it in the settings we offer to children and their parents. We need to understand what we can do to ensure that children are learning and developing in these settings.

This chapter will be interactive in the sense that you will be given some case studies to read followed by some questions to answer. In this way you are invited to interact with what you read. Do attempt to have a go at answering the questions. In many cases you will find there is no right or wrong answer. A lot of what we do in our work is informed guesswork. This applies particularly where we are trying to focus on what the child is doing or what interest the child is following. The only person who knows the answer to this for sure is the child, and we have no way of getting inside the child's head. So we have to pay close attention, use what we know about how children learn and then make an educated guess.

Here is an example:

> Maria (who is four years old) is working in the technology area of her nursery. It is well equipped with both tools and materials. She spends a long time choosing the materials to use. She selects six corks, six milk-bottle tops and an egg carton. She sticks a cork in each space of the egg carton and then sticks a bottle top on top of each cork. She takes it over to the nursery nurse and proudly announces that she has made a typewriter.

*What do you think Maria is particularly interested in? Have a guess.*

There are a number of things you might have said. You might have said that Maria was particularly interested in the number 6, or that she was exploring the concept of one-to-one correspondence by putting one thing on top of another. Or you might even have said that she was interested in putting one thing inside of or on top of another, so perhaps she was exploring position.

We have no way of knowing for sure and the only way in which we can test out our guesses is to make some comment to the child and then assess her reaction. In the real situation from which the example was drawn, the nursery nurse said to Maria, 'I see that you got six corks and six bottle tops and you stuck a cork in each of the six spaces of the egg carton'. Maria beamed at her and immediately decided to make another 'typewriter'. You might like to hazard a guess as to what the child's reaction might have been if the adult, instead of commenting on what she had achieved, had asked her to count the corks or bottle tops. What the nursery nurse is doing here is to scaffold Maria's learning by helping her to become aware of what she has done and achieved. We discussed this in Chapter 1.

## Setting up the environment

Piaget, you will remember, believed that the essential role of the adult was to provide a stimulating environment in which the child could learn and develop. This is certainly the starting point for good early years provision and one to which you have probably already paid a lot of attention. In this section we will explore what you might provide in terms of resources and activities, and how you can ensure that what you provide meets the learning needs of the children.

Not all children are in the fortunate position of Maria in the example above. Many children do not attend well-equipped nurseries, but find themselves in church halls, village halls, draughty rooms, upstairs in someone's front room in a block of flats or in the annex to the local community centre. Not all providers have limitless resources, so what you provide and how you provide it become even more important than they do in the well-funded centre. Do remember that children do not need access to vast numbers of expensive toys in order to learn but there are certain fundamental things all providers should strive to offer. Not all are expensive and many can be found in the homes of parents or be gathered together from jumble sales or car boot sales. If you have parents who are handy and willing to offer their services, they can help by making clothes or home-corner furniture or a host of other things. Essentials include books, writing and drawing and painting materials, things to build with, sand and water, and things to encourage domestic and imaginative play.

Ideally your setting should strive to organise the materials, toys and equipment in such a way that children can make their own choices and be independent in their play. Not only does this fit well with what we have learned about how young children learn but it also releases you for more vital things than finding the scissors or getting the puzzle out of a cupboard. Try and find low storage units and organise your equipment into these. There are many produced by educational suppliers, but these are often expensive. Cheaper ways are just as good: things like baskets or plastic storage tubs. It is also a good idea both organisationally and educationally to make sure that each basket or tub is labelled with both word and picture. Doing this helps children know where to find and put things and introduces children to the written word in a meaningful context.

Here is how one playgroup organised its resources:

> We went out and bought a set of plastic containers and then invited the children to help us sort the toys out. They put Lego in one, the train set in another, the farm animals in a third and so on. I then sat with the children and wrote labels. The children were really interested in what I was doing and I noticed that they wrote their own labels for the next few days. Then I asked them to help me cut out pictures of the objects and stick these next to the name. Some children wanted to draw pictures of the toys and so some labels have got a word, a photograph and a child's drawing. We thought it was going to be absolute chaos the first time we set the containers out on the floor in the morning before the children arrived – and it was. But that only lasted for one or two mornings. After that the children settled down – I guess they realised that this was how things were going to be every day so they didn't have to rush from one container to another. Now they are much more able to choose what to do and often a child will come in, go straight to one container and spend the whole morning playing with great concentration. The other really good thing that has happened is that the children get much more involved in tidying up now. It is like a game for them and they are getting better and better at sorting things out.

Having organised your resources it is time to think about how to offer children learning activities in familiar and meaningful contexts. You will remember how important it is for young children to be able to build on their previous experience and to see the point of what they are doing. Situations, drawn from children's lives, can easily be set up in your group and will offer children important learning activities as they play. The most obvious of these is some sort of area where domestic play can take place – in other words, a home corner. Do remember that the homes children come from will vary and you will want to include in your home corner some artefacts and objects which will be familiar to the children in your group.

Here is one example:

> Our old home corner was very small and we found that the children were not really playing very well in it. We sat down after nursery one day and had a real go at working out what was going wrong. We decided that the children were bored with the things in there and we noticed that the boys

hardly went in there at all and our Turkish children would go in, play for a few seconds and then leave. So we decided to ask the parents to help out. The Turkish mothers brought in a Turkish coffee pot and some dressing up clothes. One mother brought in a Turkish newspaper. Then one of the black mothers commented that all our dolls were white, so we went out and bought a black doll. One of the staff thought about bringing in an old toolbox and some 'Do It Yourself' magazines. We got the children to help us rearrange things to make the area bigger. Since then – and that is at least six months ago – the children have been playing in there with much greater concentration and we notice many more children doing things like pretending to read the newspapers or to write messages and playing many more roles while acting out complex sequences.

It seems obvious that where children encounter a range of materials to play with their play will become increasingly complex and engrossing. If you have things like knives and forks in your home corner do try and have complete sets of these – say four knives and four forks. This will help the children in their understanding of numbers and allow them to imitate some of the roles they see their families play at home. Do remember to reflect the range of cultures in your group and to respect them. Not all families use knives and forks, for example. In some cultures food is eaten using the hands, in others people use tools like chopsticks.

You might also want to consider meeting the differing needs of young children in terms of role play. Very young children will spend a long time acting out the domestic roles of family members. Ben, aged three, plays 'mummies and daddies and babies' every day. His friends, Seth and Becky, both aged four like to play the functional roles of doctor, fire-fighter, police-man, shop assistant, whilst six-year-old Phoebe plays out more fantastic roles drawn from her imagination, from stories, from television and videos.

*Think of how you would want to resource your setting to cater for such diverse needs.*

One nursery, set up a home corner and provided a range of dressing-up clothes (some made by parents together with a collection of shoes, hats, lengths of fabric) plus props (a doctor's bag, a tool kit, a picnic hamper) and turned a corner of the room into a changing role-play area (a café, a garage, a clinic). In this nursery children could play domestic, functional and fantasy roles.

Hall and Robinson (1995) give a wonderful example of how an imaginative play area can be set up to extend the opportunity for children to encounter familiar and meaningful situations beyond the home corner. They describe how a teacher took her class to visit a local garage and then set up a garage in the classroom. The teacher was particularly interested in developing children's writing skills and the children embarked on a number of exciting and unusual writing acts where they did things like fill in forms for planning permission, write letters, design posters, etc. Drawing from the meaningful context of the garage the children were able to explore the many different purposes for which people write in a way that made sense to them.

Let us pause now and summarise what has been covered so far:

- Children need a range of interesting and challenging objects and situations in which to play and learn.
- These should reflect the homes, cultures and languages of the children so that they can build on what is familiar to them.
- Children will learn best when the situations they find make sense to them and allow them to draw on what they already know and can do.
- The way in which resources are organised and labelled can encourage children to develop independence and make valid choices.
- Planning to help children become independent releases the adults so that they can spend their time observing children and interacting with them.

## Planning your activities

In many nurseries and playgroups the adults tend to offer the basic things like sand and water, construction and home-corner play each day, together with a number of 'table-top' activities – things like jigsaw puzzles, cutting and sticking and junk modelling. This type of planning reflects planning without considering the individual needs of the children and sometimes means that the children become fixed in their play and may become bored and troublesome. Let us refer back to some of what we covered in the first chapter and remind ourselves of what Vygotsky called the 'Zone of Proximal Development'. He said that what children can do with help is far more than they can do unaided. The implication of this is that we need to be aware of what the child can do alone and then help the child to make the next leap in learning.

But how can you do this? You cannot, of course, closely study each of thirty children every day to assess their present level and think of what you can do to take each child's learning forward. This would be a physical and intellectual impossibility. What you can do, however, is to select a number of children to observe closely each day or even to observe one area of your room and take note of how the children play and learn in that area.

Here are two examples to illustrate ways of doing this:

At the end of each day the staff gather together for a brief, but focused summary of the day's events. In this playgroup each staff member is a key worker for a number of children and it is these children he or she focuses on. Of course he or she may not focus on each of these children every day, but will keep careful notes to ensure that no child is forgotten or overlooked.

Maria, a parent volunteer, comments that Jordan has been unsettled and weepy and suggests that it may be the presence of the new baby that is upsetting her. The group decided that they will set up a baby clinic in the home corner area and spend a few minutes discussing what materials and equipment they will need and how they will gather this together.

The group leader, Alicia, says she thinks that four-year-old Hamish is on the verge of reading. She observed him retelling the story of 'Not Now Bernard' and actually pointing to the words as he did so. She volunteers to take a group of the older children (those who are interested, including Hamish, she hopes) to make a 'Big Book' version of the story. The children can do the illustrations and she will model the writing by doing it in front of them. She can invite individual children to guess what letter a word starts with or to write words she knows they can write.

Paulette thinks that three-year-old Sukvinder is including Urdu symbols in her 'writing'. She suggests inviting Sukvinder's mother in to sit in the writing corner and maybe write a letter in Urdu. She will make sure that there is writing paper, envelopes and stamps in the writing area.

Alicia says that four-year-old Darren is very interested in circles. He has been drawing them, making circular movements out in the garden and including circles in all his attempts at writing. She wants to put out a lot of circular shapes in the junk modelling area and observe what Darren does with these.

You will see that in this example the adults have been paying close attention to the children in order to decide how to help them in their learning. In the next example you will find the staff focusing more on what they have provided and using this as the basis for planning:

In this nursery each member of staff takes responsibility for setting up a number of activities and then spends time in them observing the children at play.

Lettie says that she had put a number of plastic containers in the water tray. 'Some of the children were filling them up with water and then pushing them to the bottom of the water tray to try and make them sink. I'm going to put the same containers in the water tomorrow, but I'm also going to include some stones. I want to see if the children try putting the stones in the containers and see what happens.'

Julian says that he read a group of children 'The Jolly Postman' and that they were really interested in the letters. He is going to put writing paper and envelopes out in the writing area and is going to rescue the post-box they had around at Christmas time. The nursery head suggests that he might like to base himself in the writing area and be seen by the children actually writing a letter himself.

Natasha has been observing the home corner and says that she feels that the children are really stuck in their play. They seem to act out the same sequences every day. 'I am going to bring in something new to see if that changes the play', she says. 'Why don't you set up the home corner in the nursery by putting an old toaster on the table together with some tools from the woodwork area?' suggests the nursery head.

A number of important points have been raised by these examples. In the first place, it is clear that in order to plan for learning and development you have to pay close attention to what children are doing and what they are interested in. In the second place, it is worth remembering that children do need long periods of time in order to get deeply involved in what they are doing. If you divide up your day into short periods of 'work' and 'play' you make this impossible. Further, children sometimes need to explore something not just over one day, but over several. In the second example you will have noticed that Lettie was not going to put something completely different in the water on the following day. She was going to let the children continue their exploration of whether or not the plastic containers would sink or not, but she was going to add something new to the existing activity. Now this is a vital point for all nursery- and reception-class practitioners. Where children are interested in exploring something, adding something new or even taking something away from the activity will offer the children an intellectual challenge and encourage them to further their explorations.

*Can you think of how the addition of stones to the water tray would offer the children a cognitive challenge? Or would you prefer to put completely different things in the water the next day?*

Lettie, possibly without knowing it, is operating the theory of 'Match' devised by McVicker Hunt. He believed that children will be helped in their learning when they are offered something new in a situation, but he emphasised that the gap between the old and the new must be neither too big nor too small. Where the gap between what the child is doing or exploring and the new situation is too big, the child cannot make the cognitive leap involved. Where the gap is too small, there is no intellectual challenge and the child will not be learning. Lettie believed that the children were exploring whether or not the containers, filled with water, would sink. By offering them stones to put inside the containers she was helping them realise something about weight and buoyancy. Had she decided to remove the plastic containers and put just some stones in the water she would not have allowed the children to make the link between what they had been doing (filling the containers) and the new activity. The theory of 'Match' is a very useful one for all those working with young children and is certainly worth bearing in mind when planning activities.

You will see the link between the theory of 'Match' and the work of Vygotsky. The introduction of the novel object or activity helps the child move from where he or she is now to a higher plane of learning and understanding.

Often, when practitioners are asked why they have provided an activity for children – something like 'cutting and sticking' for example – they respond by saying things like 'Well, the children really love it'.

*In light of what you have read so far do you think that this is an appropriate or adequate response?*

Children like all sorts of things. They like eating sweets and drinking Coca Cola and watching TV. This does not mean that these things are good for them. As nursery- and reception-class practitioners our goals must be to enhance children's learning and development, and all activities should be planned with some valid learning goal in mind. If you are planning a cutting and sticking activity your reason might be to help develop children's use of fine tools. When you plan your activities on the basis of what you have observed about the children you will almost inevitably have a learning goal in mind.

Let us now summarise this section:

- Activities need to be planned to meet the learning needs of children.
- Adults need to pay careful attention to what children are doing in order to take their learning forward.
- Practitioners need to work as a team in order to share their observations and plan together. This is both efficient and informative. Sharing information and planning together brings about an element of continuity and a sense of shared values.
- Introducing something new (either by bringing in a novel object or by removing something) can take learning forward as long as the gap between the old and the new is carefully matched.
- Children need extended periods of time in which to explore. This allows them to follow their own interests and solve the problems they set themselves in their play.
- The best planning does not mean offering something different every day. Children may need to do the same things over and over again.

## Intervening and interacting

It is a sunny Monday morning and all the children are out in the garden area. Some are playing in the sandpit, some are on the climbing frames, and some are racing round on bikes and trikes. The adult who is on 'duty' is sitting on a chair where she has a good view of all the activities. She is drinking a cup of tea and, every so often, yells a warning. Occasionally children come over to her to be comforted or to ask for something. When asked what her role is, she confidently replies that she is there in order to ensure that the children play safely. Her role is that of supervisor.

It is obvious that children's safety must be a prime concern and practitioners must do everything they can to ensure this. But since nurseries are about learning and development, the role of the adult is much more important than merely supervision. It is about more than providing a stimulating and challenging environment. It is about more than observing the children and planning activities to help them move ahead in their learning. All of these roles are important, but most important of all is what the adult does in interacting with children.

All children are born into a social world – a world in which they have dealings and interactions with a range of people. From birth children are involved in interactive acts with adults and others. Wells (1986) believes that children have to interact, especially through speech, because of their urge to communicate their desires and needs explicitly. Maxwell (1996) believes that this urge extends to a need to be close, to experience warmth and acceptance.

For Wells interaction is like the act of throwing a ball to a small child:

> First ensure the child is ready with arms cupped to catch the ball, throw gently and accurately so that it lands squarely in the child's arms. When it is the child's turn to throw, the adult must be prepared to run wherever the ball goes.
>
> (Wells 1986, p. 50)

You will recognise in this example just how much responsibility for an effective interaction rests with the adult who is the more experienced partner in the reciprocal exchange. Wells goes on to say:

> if the adult and child are to succeed in elaborating a shared meaning over a number of turns the adult has to make the effort to understand the child's intended meaning and to extend it in terms that the child can understand.
>
> (Wells 1986, p. 17)

This is the essence of effective interaction. Let us try and draw out the meaning more clearly. By 'shared meaning' Wells is talking about both parties – adult and child – paying attention to the same thing. The adult has to pay close attention to what it is the child is exploring in order that his or her interaction with the child can be focused on that. Adults sometimes have their own agenda in mind and when working with a child take the opportunity to teach the child something – the names of colours, numbers and shapes for example. But the child may be paying attention to something much more complex, and if the adult is wrong in her guess about the child's focus of attention the interaction breaks down.

Here are some examples. In each case say first what you believe the child is paying attention to and then suggest what you might do or say. Do remember that there are no right or wrong answers.

Jonas has been playing in the construction area every day for well over a week. Each time he constructs something he pays a great deal of attention to ensuring that his construction is symmetrical.

*What might you say to him? And what might you introduce next into the construction area?*

You notice that Rehana has taken a long strip of paper from the writing area and has gone over to the children's coat pegs and is laboriously copying each child's name in a list on this piece of paper.

*What might you say to her? And what might you do next to foster her development in this area?*

You have been doing some number songs with a group of children and you notice that three-year-old Bernie knows all the words and, what is more, uses her fingers when she is counting down.

*What might you say to her? And what activities might you offer her next?*
*How did you get on with doing this? You might like to compare your responses with some gathered from practitioners in the area.*

In the case of Jonas and his symmetrical buildings, one nursery worker said 'I would certainly use the word "symmetrical" in my response. I would say something like, "My goodness, Jonas. Every time you make something it is the same on both sides. We call that symmetrical." I might then bring a mirror into the construction area and see what he makes of that. Or I could put out some folded paper and see if he is interested in something like "blot" paintings.'

In the case of Rehana making a list of names one nursery nurse said, 'I would assume (perhaps wrongly) that Rehana was making a register. She sees us walking round each morning with a register, ticking off names. So, assuming she is drawing on this experience, I might try and just put in words what I think she is doing. I'd say "You're making a register, Rehana, just like the one I use in the mornings to check that the children are here." By doing this I would validate what she is doing and help her become conscious of what she already knows. If I noticed that she could actually recognise some of the names (and I am pretty sure she could) I might get her to help me check the register the next day. Or I could put out an empty register book and see what she does with that. In the longer term I would perhaps make a book for her in which we could include the names she recognises – like a song the children know: something like "Poor Jenny sits a weeping".'

In the case of three-year-old Bernie and her knowledge of numbers one playgroup worker said, 'I would comment on what she already knows, perhaps by saying something like "You know all the words of the songs, Bernie, and you are using your fingers to count down. That's what I do, isn't it? And I sometimes use the children as well." I just want to draw her attention to her achievements. I would carry on doing number songs and maybe make her a book of one of them. She could help by doing the drawings or by sticking things in.'

If you think about how you interact with other people – your friends or colleagues or family – you will realise that all of your interactions involve relating about something. It may be about who is going to set up the garden equipment in the morning or about what film you are going to see or about who is collecting the children from school. Bruner's research in 1980 showed that most of the interactions between teachers and children in schools focused on managerial issues and were primarily concerned with teachers responding to children's achievements with comments like 'good boy!' or 'well done!' Bruner suggests that those involved with children would do better to try and tune into what children are doing in more supportive ways. With older children interactions might involve discussing with children aspects of the task in which they have been involved. Whatever the interaction, the response of the adult gives the child some idea of the adult's views of the child, of learning, of the world. In other words interactions are about more than the child's behaviour or performance: they are part of the process of exchanging views, sharing meanings and scaffolding learning.

Let us now summarise what has been said in this section:

- Children learn through interaction with more experienced learners – either older children or adults.
- Interaction involves the sharing of meaning and requires the adult to pay close attention to the child's concerns in order that the child can be helped to make the next step.
- The role that adults play is complex, involving them in planning activities, talking to children, listening to children, observing children, thinking about what the children are doing, interacting.
- Adults should play a role that is more than merely supervising children's play.

- Children's learning can be scaffolded by the adult reflecting back to the child what the child already knows and can do. This helps the child become conscious of his or her own achievements.

## Guided participation

Barbara Rogoff (1990) is an American researcher who has done some interesting work on the role of adults in extending the learning of young children. She clearly builds on much of the work of Vygotsky and Bruner but takes a broader socio-cultural view, reflecting her own research with different communities. She sees that all children are born into a world where they quickly become tied into a system of relationships with others – their caregivers, their siblings, their peers, and so on. These more mature learners are already involved with all the activities of their culture and they induct the new infant into these. It is a two-way collaborative process with the children wanting to participate and to increase their understanding and the adult seeking to develop shared understanding.

It is quite difficult to see how this is different from scaffolding. Rogoff argues that this guided participation (as she calls it) is something done in all societies and that it does not involve direct teaching and often not even contact or conversation. What happens is that children are involved in the routines and rituals of daily life and through this, alongside the more experienced learners, come to be part of a shared culture.

She argues that guided participation appears throughout the world.

> Caregivers and children make arrangements for children's activities and revise children's responsibilities as they gain skill and knowledge. These arrangements and adjustments facilitate children's extension of their existing knowledge to encompass new situations. With the guidance of those around them, children participate in cultural activities that socialise them in skilled roles.
>
> (Rogoff 1990, p. 111)

You may be interested in some of the examples she cites, particularly when you consider how to understand and support the learning of younger children.

> Maria is reading 'Ten in the Bed' with twenty-month-old Efraim. He joins in to chant some numbers, showing that he has appropriated familiar routines involving counting.

> Valerie, who is not yet two, picks up her table mat to show the family, but she holds it face down. Her parents do not comment but her four-year-old sister gently tells her that it is upside down. Valerie looks down at the mat and turns it round so that it faces her family.

Children in a South African nursery class routinely fasten their dolls to their backs using strips of cloth.

An eleven-month-old child in Zaire cuts a fruit with a machete, watched by a relative.

*Can you see from these examples how both adults and other children induct children into the routines and rituals of their culture? Can you also see how important it is for those working with young children to have some knowledge of and sensitivity to the similarities and variations within and between cultural practices?*

It is clear that the role of the adult in supporting and extending children's learning is a complex one. Adults working with young children need to be knowledgeable about how young children learn best and to be sensitive in their interactions with both children and their carers. A recent trend in some countries of calling all those who work with young children 'facilitators' is concerning. The use of this term implies that the role is limited to facilitating learning, and, as we have seen in this chapter, it is about much more than that. As an adult working with young children you will often be facilitating their learning, but you will also be planning for it, monitoring it, intervening in it to take learning forward. You will be listening, watching, considering, taking notes and making decisions based on your own knowledge of child development and of individual children. The vital role of the adult will be returned to time and again throughout this book.

## References

Bruner, J. (1980) *Under Five in Britain*, London, Grant McIntyre.

Hall, N. and Robinson, A. (1995) *Exploring Writing and Play in the Early Years*, London, David Fulton.

Maxwell, S. (1996) 'Meaningful Interaction', in S. Robson and S. Smedley (eds), *Education in Early Childhood*, London, David Fulton.

Rogoff, B. (1990) *Apprenticeship in Thinking: Cognitive Development in Social Context*, Oxford, Oxford University Press.

Wells, G. (1986) *The Meaning Makers*, London, Hodder and Stoughton.

# Chapter 3

# The early years curriculum

## The Foundation Stage

In September 2000 a Foundation Stage, covering the education of children in all settings from the age of three until the end of the reception year, was introduced in England. It followed many years of heated debate and discussion, as early years' experts tried to persuade successive governments of the importance of high-quality education in the early years. Until the introduction of the Foundation Stage children started formal education on entering the reception class, and for many children this was at the age of only four. We have looked earlier at the effects of formal education too soon and seen how it can damage children's dispositions to learning. Curious children stop being curious as they realise that their curiosity is not valued: instead they are asked to learn things by rote, colour in worksheets and generally be passive in many learning situations.

England also has had the dubious honour of being one of the poorest providers for children before the compulsory starting age of school at five. Using arguments about the importance of parental choices successive governments have resisted advice about providing state-funded nurseries, opting instead for a plethora of childminders, playgroups, crèches and other part-time, private, charitable or voluntary-sector funded facilities. This brings about many difficulties in terms of quality, training, conditions of work for staff, and equity in terms of what children experience before they enter school. In ill-conceived attempts to address some of these issues – notably to try and introduce a curriculum for three- to four-year-olds – 'The Desirable Outcomes for Children's Learning on Entering Compulsory Education' was introduced in January 1996. This set out to specify goals for children's learning on entering compulsory schooling (very often, as we have said, at the age of just four) when they were immediately introduced to Key Stage 1 of the National Curriculum.

Continuing pressure from lobby groups forced the new Labour government to think again and the result is the Foundation Stage. Although it draws on many of the principles which had underpinned the 'Desirable Outcomes' it goes further in some respects. There are still aspects of the new legislation which cause some concern. Nonetheless it is clearly a significant landmark in funded education – even though much of the funding only applies to a half-time place for children – i.e. two and a half hours a day.

## The aims of the Foundation Stage

All those working with children during the Foundation Stage are expected to *plan activities and experiences* for them to help them develop and learn. The *progress of each child should be monitored* to ensure that it is satisfactory and there is a *focus on the early identification of children who may have special needs* that may require specific provision, such as specialist teaching, support within the setting or adapted equipment. Early identification of special needs is expected to avoid children experiencing failure in formal schooling.

A *broad curriculum is proposed, not arranged in traditional subjects, but in learning areas*, very similar to those identified in the 'Desirable Outcomes'. Throughout the curriculum there is emphasis on developing, fostering and supporting children's

- *personal, social and emotional well-being* by ensuring that there are thought-out procedures for settling new children in and creating an ethos that fosters self-esteem and a positive self-image in all children;
- *positive dispositions and attitudes* to their learning;
- *social skills*, helping children to learn to cooperate and work harmoniously alongside and with one another;
- *persistence and attention skills*, particularly the ability to get deeply involved in and concentrate on self-chosen individual tasks or in group play;
- *language and communication*, with an emphasis on children talking and communicating to one another and to adults, refining their language skills in an ever-widening range of situations;
- *reading and writing*, with an emphasis on helping children explore the world of stories and print by providing books to explore and situations to use words and text in increasingly controlled ways;
- *mathematics*, with opportunities to develop an understanding of number and measurement, shape and space and pattern and to use the language of mathematics with increasing fluency and accuracy;
- *knowledge and understanding of the world* so that children can pose questions and solve problems, experiment, hypothesise, express their ideas and find out about places and people significant to them;
- *physical development* which offers opportunities for children to develop fine and gross motor control and to understand something about how their bodies work and what they can do to be safe and healthy;

- *creative development* where children can express their feelings and thou and ideas through art and music, movement and dance, imaginative role play, design and technology.

The *important role of parents* in their young children's education and care is emphasised and parents are seen as partners in their children's care and education. This puts the onus on practitioners to set up a two-way exchange with parents, showing respect for the values and knowledge of the parents, listening carefully to them, communicating with them and keeping them informed.

The DfEE had published *Early Learning Goals* in October 1999 and these were defined as what each child should understand, know and be able to do at the end of the Foundation Stage. These goals were elaborations of the government's earlier 'Desirable Outcomes', and Nick Tate (Chief Executive of the Qualifications and Curriculum Authority) said,

> The early learning goals set high expectations for the end of the Foundation Stage, but expectations that are achievable for most children who have followed a relevant curriculum.
>
> (Tate in DfEE and QCA 2000, Foreword)

Later in this book we will be looking at these goals and see whether they are achievable – and desirable – for young children.

## The principles underpinning the Foundation Stage and their implications

For many playgroups and nursery classes, crèches and nursery schools there will be little that is new or challenging in the principles that follow. But as you read through them think about how a teacher in a reception class might feel.*

> *Effective Education requires both a relevant curriculum and practitioners who understand and are able to implement the curriculum requirements.*

> *Effective Education requires practitioners who understand that children develop rapidly during the early years – physically, intellectually, emotionally and socially.*

---

*In this chapter and those that follow the early-learning goals are displayed in italic script and centred on the page.

At Amandla Primary School the coming of the Foundation Stage forced the staff to re-examine their practice and the way in which the school was organised. Here are some of the things they decided to do in the first year of the Foundation Stage:

It was decided to set up an Early Years Unit, made up of the nursery and the reception class.

- The head teacher looked closely at the existing qualifications of staff and allocated two teachers to the unit – one the existing nursery teacher and one a teacher in Year 1 but with a young child of her own and developing an interest in early learning. She then allocated two nursery nurses to the unit. Both had relevant training.
- The head teacher planned an INSET programme and decided that although this was aimed primarily at the staff in the new unit, she could usefully make it available to all staff so that everyone would have a better understanding of certain points:
  - young children learn primarily through play and by having direct experience;
  - language is very important in the early years;
  - young children learn holistically and not in subjects;
  - what they learn should make human sense to them and they should see the purpose of what they are doing;
  - outdoor and indoor play are equally important.
- The head teacher planned some follow-up training to help the staff make early identification of children with special needs.
- Staff training on observation and assessment was compulsory for all staff.

*Did you identify any problems?*

A group of teachers and nursery nurses immediately highlighted the following issues:

- For many reception classes there is no dedicated outdoor play space and children end up having 'playtime' rather than having free access to outdoor play, as in the nursery.
- The nursery nurses wanted to know if there was some way in which their specialist training could be used. Could they lead staff training on observation, for example?

*Practitioners must ensure that all children feel included, secure and valued.*

*Parents and practitioners should work together in an atmosphere of mutual respect within which children can have security and confidence.*

Amandla Primary School has close links with several providers of care and education in the local community. One of these is Rainbow Playgroup which functions in the local church hall. Rainbow Playgroup is highly regarded in the local community and parents say that they feel very welcomed there and have no trouble in talking to the staff about anything that concerns or interests them.

The head teacher of Amandla decides to send the Early Years Unit staff to visit and take notes. When they return to the school they are invited to report back their findings to the whole staff. This is what they say:

> Rainbow Playgroup takes in many children who speak languages other than English. The main language group is Sylheti, just as it is at Amandla School. The playgroup has a practitioner who speaks Sylheti and lives in the local community. She knows many of the families and knows something about what their fears and needs are. She understands how nervous they might be about going to talk to 'teachers' and how difficult it is for them to communicate in formal settings in English. She sees herself as the link person between the families, the staff at the playgroup and outside agencies. She goes with parents to see the speech therapist, for example. She works with the staff to ensure that the images and objects the children encounter reflect people and homes like their own. She helps the staff avoid stereotyping the children and their families.

*What do you think so far? Do you think that Amandla School can learn from this?*
The playgroup operates a keyworker scheme – something that is completely new to the teachers and to one of the nursery nurses. In this system each child is allocated to one key person who is the person who will take main responsibility for the child's well-being. This keyworker visits the homes of the children who are due to come in (always by appointment and with approval!): she explains to the family what the routines of the playgroup are and helps plan how the child will be settled in. The playgroup tries to make the settling-in arrangements as flexible as possible to meet the needs of their working parents, but they do tell new parents that they must arrange some time to stay with the child at first since the needs of the child are primary. The keyworker is the one who maintains records of the child's progress (although all practitioners may contribute to this) and she or he is the person who liaises with the primary school when the time to transfer comes.

*No child should be excluded or disadvantaged because of ethnicity, culture or religion, home language, family background, special educational needs, disability, gender or ability.*

This is such an important principle that we will examine it on its own.

The staff of Rainbow Playgroup felt that they could learn much from Amandla Primary School about issues relating to inclusion. They knew that several of the staff had attended courses about this and that the school was particularly well resourced. So three members of the playgroup staff went and spent a day at the school in the new unit and on their return they organised a meeting in the church hall and invited parents and people from the local community.

Here are some of the things that impressed them:

- There was a really welcoming entrance hall with greetings written in a number of languages, photographs of all the staff with their names, a suggestion box and a number of books made for parents with photographs of some of the things that happened in the unit and with texts in a number of languages.
- In the reception class and the nursery there were a number of alphabets and scripts on display and the children's names appeared all over the place. The reception class teacher explained that they sometimes asked older siblings to help write the children's names in the script used in the home.
- There were folders in each of the rooms containing a profile for each child and in this any practitioner could put observation notes or comments. Parents could read these and also write in them if they wanted to. There were also some examples of children's work with comments saying what they showed about the child's learning and development.
- They fell in love with the home corner which was divided up into rooms and each room had resources to reflect the variety of homes the children came from. So in the kitchen were chapatti pans and chopsticks and knives and forks: in the bedroom were dolls of different colours and genders: in the sitting room was a television, a computer, magazines, a tool kit and a do-it-yourself manual.
- The room was not at all cluttered and they noticed that a child on crutches could move easily around the room. The nursery nurse explained that they had removed two tables to allow for this and that the children happily worked on the floor.
- The nursery and reception class were very well resourced when it came to books and the playgroup practitioners were very pleased to see books showing children and families as varied as those in the community. Apart from storybooks and picture books there were books about children in wheelchairs: about birth and death: about different festivals: about women and men doing a wide range of jobs and sharing in childcare.

Altogether they felt rather envious of the wide resources available, but also inspired by some of the things they had seen.

Many of the things they saw supported the next principl

*For children to have rich and stimulating experiences, the learning*
*should be well planned and well organised.*

Amandla Early Years Unit staff plan like this. Every member of staff is asked to observe one activity over a week – perhaps the sand, or the water, or an activity in the home corner, for example. They keep notes on what they observe and at the end of each day they all gather together for a brief, focused meeting. At this meeting they share what they noticed. They talk about who played in the area (and who didn't!): what they did and what they were paying attention to. On the basis of this they decide what they will do with that area the next day. Will they put it out in exactly the same way? Will they add something or take something away? In addition to this they each follow four target children for the week. These may be their key children or may not. They observe them, make notes and put these in their profiles to be looked at by the keyworker at the end of the week.

Rainbow Playgroup plan to meet the interests and needs of individual children. This is an extremely time-consuming process. Each child has a chart on which his or her particular interests are noted down. Parents are involved in helping with this and activities are planned to meet the needs of the children. Of course the staff cannot possibly plan one activity for each child, but they have noticed that offering open-ended activities will draw in many children. An example is of a shoe shop they set up recently in response to one child's obsession with his shoes. By providing pairs of shoes of different sizes, carrier bags and old shoe boxes, fake cheque books and a till, and a foot-measure they have managed to involve almost all the children in some engrossing play.

*How do you plan at your workplace? What, if anything, can you learn from these*
*models?*

*To be effective an early years curriculum should be carefully structured.*

*There should be opportunities for children to engage in activities planned by adults*
*and also those that they plan or initiate themselves.*

*Well-planned, purposeful activity and appropriate intervention by practitioners*
*will engage children in the learning process.*

*What do you understand by the words 'structured', 'purposeful' and 'appropriate*
*intervention'?*

Here is what some childcare practitioners and teachers said:

- I think structured means that everything should be planned, although the planning should be flexible enough to be put aside to follow exciting events (for example, a snowy day) or children's interests.
- Before the Foundation Stage was introduced I used to think that 'structured' meant working towards the learning outcomes of Key Stage 1 in all areas of the curriculum. Now I know that in the reception class I need to think of structuring experiences and activities to cover all the areas of learning and to plan for learning inside and out. This is quite a culture shift!
- I used to think that when we talked of 'structure' we meant adult-directed activities. I now know that if we, as a team, plan on the basis of what we have observed children to be doing and paying attention to we can create a stimulating learning environment where children can make their own plans and carry them through. For us in reception class this is a difficult idea. It means we have to 'lose control' and hand it over to the children. At first this felt dangerous, but now we are seeing the benefits.
- We had a long discussion about the word 'purposeful' and it was quite heated. Some people thought that if we gave children a worksheet to complete it was purposeful and the purpose was to complete it – i.e. to follow instructions. But most of us agreed that purposeful meant that the purpose – the point of doing it – should be apparent to the child. So matching shapes on a worksheet might not have a clear purpose, but putting things away in the right place (matching them to their labels) might.
- We all felt confident that we intervene in children's learning. We thought that we did this by questioning children and by commenting when they have done something well. After some training about intervention we have become more critical of what we do and begun to tape-record and video ourselves to see what we actually do. We now believe that it is sometimes appropriate just to let children be – to talk and explore and try things out; sometimes we need to step in to help a child who is struggling; sometimes we need to use very relevant language to take learning forward and mostly what we need to do is help children realise what they have achieved and then take them forward. So intervening is very closely tied to scaffolding.

*Practitioners must be able to observe and respond appropriately to children.*

Observation is a key part of the role of anyone working with young children. We will talk more about this in a later chapter. For now you might want to read part of this observation of a child made by Lynne Bennett as part of her training:

> Daniella is 3 years 3 months old and is playing in the home corner with two other children . . .
>
> Daniella comes into the house, holding a shopping basket and doll and says 'Big sister is going shopping and you look after the baby please.' She puts the doll on the sofa and says 'She is very sick. Put her there (points to a cushion on a sofa) and take her hat off. Her eyes are flashing and her ears are sore'. She puts a spoon in the doll's ear and makes the noise 'sloosh' . . .
>
> (Bennett 1998, p. 6)

Lynne has written down everything that happened; everything she saw and heard. She didn't add any comments or judgements of her own. At the end of the day she read through the observation and tried to use it to help her in her planning.

*What would you say that Daniella knows? What do you think she is interested in? What might you plan as an activity or learning area to take her interests forward?*

You can read more about the Foundation Stage in the document entitled *Curriculum Guidance for the Foundation Stage*, published by the DfEE and QCA in 2000. You can also access the QCA website at the following address: www.qca.org.uk. We will return to the Foundation Stage throughout the rest of this book.

Let's summarise what has been said so far:

- the Foundation Stage is potentially an extremely significant development in provision for young children;
- it affects children in all settings from the age of three until they leave the reception class;
- it emphasises the fact that young children learn best through hands-on, self-chosen, direct experience alone, with peers or with an adult;
- it recognises that young children do not learn in subjects and that learning is holistic;
- personal, social and emotional well-being is the basis for successful learning and development;
- all young children need access to opportunities for physical development in terms of both fine and gross motor skills;
- the curriculum should be planned to meet the needs and interests of all children and care must be taken to ensure that no child is in any way excluded or discriminated against;
- observation and monitoring of children's progress is vital, as is the early identification of those with special educational needs;
- close working partnerships with parents are key to successful early years practice;

- a quality curriculum is a planned curriculum where the planning is sufficiently flexible to be responsive to children's needs and interests;
- practitioners need to be adequately trained so that they are able to offer a quality curriculum.

We will now look at provision in some other countries in order to learn from practice that may be different from ours. If we are concerned to provide children with a curriculum that is responsive to their needs there is much we can learn from our first example – the famous nurseries in Reggio Emilia.

## Nursery provision in Reggio Emilia, Italy

In the wealthy area of northern Italy the provision of high-quality childcare and education has been a priority of all the local people since the end of the Second World War. Led by an idealist and educationalist, Loris Malaguzzi, local people obtained the resources and the support to establish a number of nurseries which are still the envy of the developed world. So much so that the number of visitors to these nurseries has had to be limited in recent years.

There are a number of features that make the provision special. Firstly, parents and other people in the local community are involved in the management of these nurseries and their words are listened to. Secondly, everything that happens is documented. Careful records are kept of every aspect of the work and these are analysed so that successful things can be replicated and unsuccessful things dropped. All the nurseries are in purpose-built facilities and the architects and planners have to take account of the social, emotional and educational needs of the children and practitioners when designing the building and the equipment to go in it. Staff have good working conditions and an ongoing programme of in-service training.

Most impressive, however, is the quality of the work of the children. Visitors are often stunned by the intensity of the children's concentration as they draw and paint, use the computers, design and construct, make and send messages to one another and explore the physical space. The philosophy of the nurseries is that childhood is important in its own right and that children should encounter a range of meaningful experiences and activities in order that they become able to represent and rerepresent what they have seen and heard and learned.

Here is an example to illustrate this:

> In a nursery in Modena a project developed around the theme of lions. In Modena the cathedral, set in a magnificent square, has stone lions outside it. All the families of Modena use the square as a meeting place and all the children regard the lions as familiar. The staff took a group of children to visit the lions. The children took with them clipboards and pencils and

they were invited to draw the lions if they wanted to. Back at the nursery a host of other activities were on offer. Some children drew the lions in pencil and then made large and brilliantly coloured paintings. Some made giant lions out of large cardboard boxes and junk materials. Some dressed up as lions and made up stories or dances. Some made lions out of clay, using tools skilfully and appropriately. In this way the children were able to represent their ideas and feelings about the lions in a range of ways. You will remember how learning involves the establishment of connections between brain cells. In this example each time a representation was made (a drawing or a model or a dance or a poem) another set of connections was established.

In another nursery in the same region the teachers (all practitioners are given the title of teacher) were concerned that children's links with the nursery might be damaged over the long summer holiday. So they gave each child a box and invited the children to put anything in the box they chose to remind them of the summer. The children were asked to bring the filled boxes back to the nursery when term resumed. One little girl had, in her box, a bus ticket. Through discussion, the staff discovered that it was the ticket she had used to go and visit her grandparents who lived at the seaside. When she was asked what she had seen at the seaside she surprised the adults by saying she had seen 'arms and legs'. They had been expecting her to say 'buckets and spades' or 'ice creams'. As sensitive and exploring teachers the adults explored further and discovered that the seaside town the little girl had visited was situated on a steep hillside and, in order to get to the beach, she had to walk down steep streets. Put yourself in the position of a four-year-old and you will realise that in doing this you are, indeed, surrounded by a forest of arms and legs. The staff started talking to the children about what was meant by the word 'crowd' and they discovered that most of the children thought that a crowd meant a group of people all going in the same direction.

*Stop at this point and consider what you might have done to take the children's understanding of a crowd further.*

Here is what the staff at the nursery above did. They first took the children out into the square so that they could be part of a crowd and notice that not all the people were going in the same direction. They then suggested that the children draw one another – from the front, from the back and in profile. They then enlarged some of the drawings and shrunk others using the photocopier. The final versions were coloured in by the children, cut out and mounted on card so that they would stand upright. The resulting collection of images was placed upright in a large box so that the children had a symbolic representation of a crowd.

...ɪκ of these Italian nursery schools is underpinned by a clear philo-
...ny which embraces many of the points outlined in the principles for high-
quality early learning. The type of curriculum that emerges from this is one
that can be described as *developmental*. Such a curriculum takes as its starting
point a dynamic view of development. This recognises that human development changes over time and with experience so that the ways in which young
children learn are recognised as different from the ways in which older
children and adults learn. Such a dynamic view also recognises the impact
of what is called 'delayed impact' which refers to the ways in which early
experience may affect later functioning, particularly with regard to the development of self-esteem, social development, feelings and dispositions. The
third aspect of a developmental viewpoint is the long-term cumulative
effect of frequent experiences. This implies that something that happens to
a young child once or twice may be beneficial in the short term, but repeated
exposure over a long period of time may have damaging effects.

These are quite difficult ideas to grasp but they are important to those of us
concerned with promoting early learning and development. Loris Malaguzzi
(personal communication, 1992) said that he knew that once children started
school they would be exposed to what he described as tedious and meaningless
tasks – things like colouring in, joining the dots, tracing their names,
completing jigsaw puzzles. He urged us:

> Look around you at the remarkable creative and original things the
> children can do and then think about how the school teachers, by ignor-
> ing all that children have already done and achieved by the time they start
> school, make the children feel stupid and ignorant and give them things
> that offer no intellectual challenge. The teachers in schools keep telling us
> that we don't 'teach' the children properly. By that they mean that we
> don't train them to do meaningless things. I say to them, 'We give
> our children a sense of their own identity, opportunities to express
> their thoughts and ideas through some of the hundred languages at
> their disposal (writing, drawing, building, designing, acting, dancing,
> singing) and we believe that we lay a foundation which will allow the
> children to get through their schooling with their attitude to learning
> and discovery undamaged. That is our job.' I say to them, 'Maybe you
> should learn from us and not expect us to prepare the children for
> years of tedium and boredom.'
>
> (Personal communication with Malaguzzi 1992)

Contrast this developmental approach with an example offered by Lilian
Katz. In an American preschool a group of four-year-olds were engaged in
what Katz describes as the 'calendar ritual'. Katz describes what happened
as follows:

With the children seated on the floor facing a large calendar showing the month of February, the teacher asks them what day it is today. They call out the days of the week in what appears to be random fashion, and by chance none offers the correct answer; which is Thursday. The teacher then asks, 'What day was it yesterday?' The same array of guesses is offered, which fortunately includes Wednesday. She responds 'That's right! So what day is it today?' Eventually she coaxes them into agreeing on the correct answer.

When she asks next for the date (the 19th) no one replies. She then asks one of the children to come forward and write the correct numbers in the appropriate empty box on the calendar. When he hesitates, she suggests that he look at the number for yesterday. Unfortunately, he looks in the box above rather than to the left of the empty one. Because it contains the number 12, the child says 13. Pointing out that he has looked 'the wrong way' the teacher asks, 'What comes after 18?' She thereby persuades him to agree on the date, which he manages to write almost legibly in the box . . .

(Personal communication with Katz 1988)

Katz points out that the children involved were far too young to understand the concept of the date, but because they were eager to please the teacher they behaved with great courtesy, attempting to produce the answer that would satisfy her. Katz goes on to say that if something like this happened to young children once or twice in the early years it would probably have no deleterious effect. But in many preschool settings in the United States and in many reception classes in schools this type of decontextualised activity happens with monotonous regularity, day in and day out. As we have said before, young children will learn from all experiences and they may learn undesirable as well as desirable things. For Katz, then, the developmental question is not so much what children can do or even how they learn. The question is rather: what *should* they do that will *best* help their learning and development in the long term? Katz urges that those working with young children pay attention not only to what is known about how young children learn, but also take heed of the effects of the long-term cumulative effects of the experiences they encounter.

For us, then, the message is that the curriculum is not only about what children should learn, but crucially how they should learn. What we, the adults, do is crucial to their learning and development in the long term.

## One way or many?

Most of the research and theory quoted here has come from a Western perspective. It is important to remember that the users of our preschool services come from a range of backgrounds, with varying expectations and differing values. In their book *Preschool in Three Cultures*, Tobin, Wu and Davidson examine an American preschool, a Japanese preschool and a Chinese preschool and their findings provide much food for thought.

In American preschools the pursuit of happiness is often one of the explicit goals, whereas Chinese preschools are regarded as places of serious learning where, if the children are happy as they learn, so much the better, but happiness is a by-product and not a goal. The Japanese preschools aim to produce children who are childlike and this means that they will often be happy but may also be angry, frustrated, lonely or selfish. The outcome of this is that Japanese children are encouraged to learn through play in a loosely planned environment where the adults stay on the fringes of children's play and do not intervene in order to support and extend learning.

It is obvious, too, that preschools in affluent societies will be better resourced and equipped than those in poorer countries. American preschools provide children with an overwhelming amount of toys, books, miniature versions of adult things (like irons and Hoovers), outdoor equipment, and so on. On the walls are children's drawings and images of 'happy' things – like cartoon characters, animals dressed like people and nursery rhymes. The question arises as to whether such an abundance of equipment is necessary for learning and development. If the answer to this question is yes, ill-equipped playgroups will feel that they have no chance to compete with their better-equipped counterparts. A Japanese preschool teacher commented as follows:

> We don't have a make-believe corner, but children in our school play lots of imaginary games. They play house and store and fireman. You don't need costumes and plastic dishes to play house. You don't need a fireman's hat to pretend you're a fireman. I don't think that children need all of those special things to play. Don't teachers in America believe children have imagination?
>
> (Tobin *et al.* 1989, p. 155)

This may be consoling for you if you are struggling to gather together all the materials and resources you see so glossily displayed in educational catalogues. It is worth bearing in mind that more than half the world's children learn and play using natural, found and real materials.

Although all parents recognise that children play, and through their play learn, many of them fall into the trap of believing that once children start in the nursery or school they should put playing away and start to 'learn for real'. One of the most difficult things practitioners have to do is to explain to parents why play is important. Practitioners can only do that if they themselves understand this and understand how play is different from work.

## References

Bennet, L. (1998) '"Her Eyes Are Flashing and Her Ears Are Sore": Making Sense of Life', in S. Smidt (ed.), *The Early Years: A Reader*, London, Routledge.

DfEE (1996) 'The Next Steps', London, DfEE.

DfEE and QCA (2000) *Curriculum Guidance for the Foundation Stage*, London, DfEE.

Early Years Curriculum Group (1992) *First Things First*, London, Boon Printers.

Elkind, D. (1986) 'Formal Education and Early Childhood Education: An Essential Difference', *Phi Delta Kappa*, May.

Katz, L. (1988) 'What Should Young Children Be Doing?', *American Educator*, Summer.

Malaguzzi, L. with Gandini, L. (1995) 'History, Ideas and Basic Philosophy', in C. Edwards *et al.* (eds), *The One Hundred Languages of Children*, London, Ablex Publishing.

School Curriculum and Assessment Authority (1996) 'Desirable Outcomes for Children's Learning on Entering Compulsory Education', London, DfEE.

Smidt, S. (ed.) (1998) *The Early Years: A Reader*, London, Routledge.

Tobin, J.J., Wu, D.Y.H. and Davidson, D.H. (1989) *Preschool in Three Cultures*, London and New Haven, Yale University Press.

# Chapter 4

# Living and communicating in a social world

The Foundation Stage is a new term used to refer to the planned programme of activities and interactions for children in all settings before they start statutory schooling and in their first year of statutory schooling. So children in nursery classes and schools, in playgroups and crèches, in day-care centres and other settings and in reception classes in schools are all following a programme designed to allow them to meet a set of early learning goals which represent what we expect children to know, do and understand when they leave the reception class. You will realise that early learning goals go beyond the earlier 'Desirable Outcomes' and need to be read and understood within the principles outlined earlier in this book. The *Curriculum Guidance* (discussed in the previous chapter) outlined six learning areas, whilst still emphasising that all learning in the Foundation Stage should be holistic. In this chapter we will look at how young children make sense of their social worlds and of the world of language, literacy and communication.

## Personal, social and emotional development

Judy Dunn (1988) says:

> Children are born into a complex social world: from infancy on, they are active participants in a world of other people – adults and children, familiar and not so familiar others. On common-sense grounds it seems reasonable to argue that it is important for them to begin to understand the intentions, feelings and actions of others who share their world and to comprehend the social rules of that world.
>
> (Dunn 1988, p. 1)

She goes on to illustrate how this takes place. Human infants are predisposed to learn about the characteristics of people. They are very attentive to shapes and patterns that are like human faces and respond to sounds similar to that of the human female voice. At the age of only two months they can differentiate between someone who wants to communicate with them from someone talking to someone else. By the age of seven or eight months babies seem really attuned to different emotional expressions in adults and they begin to play cooperative games like Peekaboo. They share in the daily routines of feeding, changing and dressing and soon begin to demonstrate that they share a communicative framework with others – waving goodbye, eye-pointing to what they want, smiling with pleasure. They are highly social and sociable beings.

Colwyn Trevarthen (1995) goes further and looks at how children come to learn about the culture into which they have been born. He asks why it is that very young children are so keen to learn the language and all the other habits and customs and rituals and beliefs of the community around them. He says that a three-year-old child is a socially aware person who can make and keep friends, who can negotiate and cooperate with many different people in many different situations. For Trevarthen young children primarily make sense by sharing. They use their emotions and the emotions of others to categorise experiences that will help them cooperate.

These views of the sociable child, busily seeking to understand the social and cultural rules and norms, can be used as the backdrop for looking at the early learning goals in this area. The goals will be grouped to help the argument.

*Continue to be interested, excited and motivated to learn.*

*Be confident to try new activities, initiate ideas and speak in a familiar group.*

We know that the human infant is intensely curious and seeks to understand all aspects of the world into which he or she is born. This curiosity which is innate is what Lilian Katz calls a positive disposition. You will remember that Katz says such dispositions should be encouraged and fostered and has demonstrated how such dispositions can be damaged through too early exposure to formal learning. Children's curiosity is most likely to be promoted when they are able to follow their own concerns or interests in a stimulating and challenging environment which offers first-hand experience, talk and appropriate adult intervention.

Here is an example given by Mary Smith (1998) to illustrate this:

> The children were interested in some bees in the centre garden. One boy wanted to know how honey was made. He suggested that they make some in the centre. Mary asked him how this could be done and he said that they needed to get together some flowers – daisies, buttercups and dandelions that were growing wild in the garden. He duly gathered these together and put them in a plastic tray. Daniel (aged 4.6) then

said 'We have to pick out the pollen from the middle of each flower' and then spent a considerable amount of time doing this. When he was satisfied that he had got all the pollen he asked Mary to get him a cup and spoon. Daniel put the pollen in the cup and stirred it around a bit. After a while Mary asked him what was happening to the pollen. 'Nothing' he replied 'we have to add apple juice and then we will have honey'.

(Smith 1998, p. 148–9)

Children's curiosity runs the risk of being damaged when they are asked to do inappropriate things – things that do not make 'human sense' to them. Before the advent of the Foundation Stage many children in reception classes were being asked to engage in rote learning, the completion of meaningless tasks and the solving of decontextualised problems. The Foundation Stage offers the possibility for learning in this year to be more rooted in activities that will maintain children's curiosity, excitement and desire to learn. Where this happens it is likely that children will have the confidence to try new activities, and within a supportive environment they are likely to speak in a familiar group as long as they know that what they say will matter to those listening to them.

*Select and use activities and resources independently.*

Children who find themselves in a well-structured and well-planned learning environment will know that they can follow their own interests and find the things they need for themselves. A well-set-out environment has a place for everything – a place that is accessible and evident to children. There are labels in the form of pictures and words. Time is spent on helping the children know what can be found where and children are expected, as part of their learning, to clear away at the end of each session. Good practitioners induct children into the rules of the setting and in doing this help children understand why rules are needed.

Here is what Ms Singh does in her reception class:

At the beginning of the year I always talk to the children about where things belong, how to put them away and why it is important to care for them. We often talk about what would happen if they leave the lids off the pens, or fold the pages of books. The children come up with rules for themselves. I don't have rules saying things like 'only four children in the sand' because it seems to me that the children can be self-regulating and will appreciate that when activities are overcrowded play is damaged. I depend on the children to sort things out for themselves and mostly they do. I find that when I don't have to be busy making sure they are keeping to imposed rules I have more time to really interact with them or observe them.

In an environment like this the development of children's independence is fostered and children learn quickly that they have the capacity to make choices, find what they need and sometimes to change their plans. Children are expected to learn through play and the adults become not managers of the resources, but promoters of children's learning and development.

*Maintain attention, concentrate and sit quietly when appropriate.*

Anyone who has paid attention to young children, knows that when they are really interested in something they are able to get deeply immersed in it and persevere and concentrate over long periods of time. Providing opportunities to do this is a vital principle of quality early years education and there is much here for those in reception classes to consider.

*Do you think the day in the reception class should consist of different 'lessons'? Do you think children should have 'playtime'? Or do you think the day should be more like a traditional nursery day – long, unbroken stretches of time in which to get deeply involved and ongoing access to outdoor play?*

Here is an example from a reception class where the teacher had brought in some plants plus magnifiers for the children to use. She had wanted them to be able to describe plants, using the magnifier to highlight particular features. The children all had English as an additional language and during the teacher's lengthy explanation they were largely silent. Then one child spotted a snail on a leaf and the teacher took the opportunity to abandon her plan and be led by the children. The little group, which had been largely passive and silent, suddenly came to life. They touched the snail, looked at it and discussed passionately whether it was dead or asleep when it withdrew into its shell. One child went off to find a programme on the computer that had snails in it whilst another chose some paper and pastels to draw a snail. The activity went on throughout the morning with children deeply engrossed.

We do, of course, want children to concentrate and maintain attention, but do we also want them to 'sit quietly when appropriate'? Children will listen to something that interests, amuses or entertains them. You have only to watch children at the theatre or watching a programme on television or listening to a story for evidence of this. We do want children to be able to do this in situations which are significant for them. In such sessions we are happy to have children contribute their own ideas and to discuss and comment to one another and to the adults. We rarely, if ever, have reason to want silence with such young children. It is, after all, more a way of controlling children than enhancing their learning and development. A danger implicit in having this as a goal is that teachers and practitioners might be tempted to teach in ways that are not entirely appropriate to young children. Defining what we mean by 'appropriate' in this goal is important and we need to consider if we want young children to sit quietly because *they* want to see and hear or if we want them to sit quietly as a means of controlling them. One obvious example is in reception classes where teachers are sometimes under pressure to introduce some of the aspects of the Literacy Hour and do this by getting children to sit in a large group, being passive, for rather too long. We will discuss this in more detail in the next chapter.

*Respond to significant experiences, showing a range of feelings when appropriate.*

*Have a developing awareness of their own needs, views and feelings and be sensitive to the needs, views and feelings of others.*

When Hannah was just five she saw the film *ET* on television and when ET appeared to have died, she wept.

*Would you regard this as an appropriate response? Do you think that young children should always be happy or are there times when it is appropriate for them to be sad or angry or jealous or scared?*

Abby came to nursery very angry for a week or so. Before that she had seemed very settled, so we asked her carer if anything had changed at home. We were distressed to find that Abby's mother had been admitted to hospital and realised that the child was displaying emotions appropriate to her distress.

Diane McClellan and Lilian Katz (1992) have developed a checklist which practitioners can use to help them understand how individual children can be supported as they grow in social skilfulness. These include the following:

- the child is usually in a positive mood;
- usually copes with rebuffs and reverses adequately;
- shows the capacity to empathise;
- displays the capacity for humour;
- does not seem to be acutely or chronically lonely.

Katz also offers practitioners ways of assessing children's 'range of affect'. What she means by this is looking to see if any child displays a range of emotions – joy, sorrow, anger, relief, etc. She argues that a child whose emotions are of low intensity may be having some difficulties which a practitioner should know about. Katz is clear that emotions we might regard as negative – such as sadness – involve the child in knowing about other associated emotions which are often positive. We feel sad when we feel not cared for or when a loved one goes away. In other words, in order to feel sad we have to know what it is to feel cared for or happy or loved.

Judy Dunn has illustrated how young children move from being egocentric, through an awareness of their own needs, views and feelings to understanding and being sensitive to the views, needs and feelings of others. A group of practitioners contributed these examples to illustrate this:

- When my daughter was three she was given a doll as a birthday present from her grandmother and she burst into tears and said, 'I really wanted a car'. She had no sense that she was upsetting her Gran. A year later she was given a copy of a book she already has. 'I've got this, Gran, but it's OK because mine is old and scruffy.' In a year she had moved on to knowing that her actions and words can have an effect on someone else and that she has the power to hurt someone's feelings.
- The children in the reception class are very protective of one another when a supply teacher visits. They always tell me when I return who cried and why and what they did to 'make it better'. I make a note of the children who comment and record these comments in their profiles as a record of their developing maturity in terms of personal, social and emotional development.

*Have a developing respect for their own cultures and beliefs and those of other people.*

*Understand that people have different needs, views, cultures and beliefs, that need to be treated with respect.*

*Understand that they can expect others to treat their needs, views, cultures and beliefs with respect.*

All our children are growing up in a rich and multicultural world. This applies to children growing up in rural areas where there are few people of other cultures as much as it does to those in inner-city, richly diverse communities. In order for children to develop respect for different cultures, beliefs and languages it is important that they encounter adults who enjoy the diversity of our society and show the languages, cultures and religions of the children equal respect. You may want to consider whether this is best done by celebrating the odd festival and occasionally offering some of the traditional foods to the children or whether it should be more deeply embedded in the everyday activities offered to the children. In other words, should Foundation Stage settings think that it is enough to celebrate Chinese New Year, for example, or do they need to go more deeply into this issue?

Here is how one London teacher, Birgit Voss, describes how she and her co-workers prepare for the coming term:

> I make a note of the different languages our little community will be using for the next four months: Gujerati, Bengali, Turkish, Urdu, Cantonese, Persian, Arabic, German and, of course, English. I check these against our present resources. We have cassette story and video story tapes in all the languages but Cantonese. We have plenty of writing samples, newspapers and magazines in Chinese as we had some Chinese-speaking children earlier. When we celebrated Chinese New Year – the Year of the Dog – we stocked up during a visit to the local Chinese supermarket. We also have appropriate clothes, fabrics and home-base equipment, and lots of pictures. The parents seemed very open, friendly and cooperative during the home visit. I am sure they would love to make some story tapes, maybe sing some songs for us. Something to organise.
>
> (Voss 1998, p. 48)

Voss goes on to explain that the children in her nursery class learn from first-hand experience by building on what they already know and states that this approach is ideally suited to the learning needs of young bilingual children. You can see how, in this example, the celebration of culture and language is embedded in the everyday activities. The home corner is equipped with artefacts, printed materials and pictures that reflect this. The books and stories and songs are available in languages additional to English. In an environment like this, children are most likely to respond with enthusiasm, interest and respect for the world around them.

Voss, who is herself bilingual, understands how powerfully one's language is tied up with one's identity and self-esteem. There is no mention of respect for languages in the early learning goals but it is deeply embedded in the principles and underpinning philosophy of the Foundation Stage.

You may be interested and, perhaps, shocked to learn how soon young children pick up negative attitudes to people from other groups. Using large fabric 'Persona' dolls, representing children from different groups, Glenda MacNaughton carried out some research with preschool children in Melbourne, Australia. She found that all the white Australian children were happy to play with the white middle-class-looking dolls and recognised them as being 'Australian'. When it came to a Vietnamese doll this was totally rejected by the children and none of them chose to play with the Aboriginal doll, although some reluctantly said it might be Australian. Deeply racist views were apparent in children under the age of six!

*Form good relationships with adults and peers.*

Children are most likely to form good relationships with adults and peers where they themselves are taken seriously, treated with respect and invited to learn in an environment which has both familiar and new things and experiences. It is interesting that there is no mention of building self-esteem in these early learning goals although, again, it is contained in the underlying principles. Many practitioners believe that this is something they strive to achieve, and something that they need to pay careful attention to is ensuring that there is no clash between the values of home and the values of the setting. Children are most likely to feel good about themselves when they are accepted and valued. Most of what children have learned when they start in any preschool setting has come from home. Where there is a clash between the values of home and those of the setting, children's confidence and self-esteem is damaged.

This raises an important and difficult question. How are practitioners expected to reconcile their values and their understanding of child development with the views and desires of parents? Eve Gregory graphically describes the experience of the teacher of a Chinese child in Northampton:

> Tony enters school smiling . . . A month later, Tony's behaviour has undergone a complete change. His smile has disappeared, replaced, in Mrs G's words, by a 'dead-pan look' which 'you can't seem to get through to'.
>
> (Gregory 1995)

In an effort to regain Tony's initial enthusiasm for school Mrs G visits the family at home, taking with her an attractive dual-language picture/story-book which she invites the family to share with him. Tony's grandfather refuses to accept the book, stating that Tony cannot have the book until he can read the words in it. Tony's grandfather goes on to show disgust at Tony's attempts to write his name in English – ToNy. In disgust, the grandfather states: 'This is from his English school. This is rubbish . . . Look. He can't even write his name yet!' The teacher, Mrs G, has a clearly thought-out philosophy about how young children learn and describes this philosophy as being 'child-centred'. The important point, Gregory believes, is that discontinuity between home and school or setting is more damaging to children's confidence and self-esteem – and hence to their learning and development – than the adoption of an accepted model of teaching. Practitioners need to listen to parents, to treat their views and experience with respect and to make sure that they are able to explain clearly why they are doing things so that family members can understand. Discontinuity between home and school does not only apply to children who have languages other than English. In her book *Ways with Words* Shirley Brice Heath (1983) showed how in one community in America some children came to school with values which matched those of the school whilst others did not. All the children were competent learners, fluent speakers of their own languages and well aware of the social rules and mores of their communities. Yet, once in school, those whose experience was different from that of the teachers and whose cultures were unfamiliar began to fail.

*Work as part of a group or class, taking turns and sharing fairly, understanding that there need to be agreed values and codes of behaviour for groups of people, including adults and children, to work harmoniously together to establish effective relationships with other children and with adults.*

Children in well-run Foundation Stage settings will have opportunities to play alone, in pairs, in small groups and sometimes to come together for large-group activities. As they do this they learn to work alongside others, sometimes sharing and taking turns. Where adults talk to them and model appropriate behaviour, they come to work out and internalise the social rules governing what is appropriate in their setting. With support they move from playing on their own to playing alongside other children. As they get older they begin to interact in their play and, by the time children have reached the age of four, many of them will be engaged in what is known as 'cooperative play'. In such play children collaborate on a shared project or topic. In your setting you will want to ensure that there are opportunities for such play. But do remember that children may continue to need to engage in solitary or parallel play beyond the Foundation Stage.

*Understand what is right, what is wrong and why.*

*Consider the consequences of their words and actions for themselves and others.*

In settings where children have opportunities to discuss classroom events and those that occur in their lives away from the setting they begin to refine their concepts of right and wrong. Read through this small example from Amandla reception class and decide what it was that the teacher (and possibly the other children) did that helped Charley consider right and wrong.

ALEX:        Miss, Charley hit me.
TEACHER:   Is that true, Charley? Did you hit Alex?
               No reply
TEACHER:   I hope you can remember that story we read yesterday, children, about the new child who was bullied at school and went home crying. Do you remember, Charley?
               No answer

TAKLIMA:   I remember that story. It was sad. I don't want anybody to hit me or bully me. I like school.

TEACHER:   I am really pleased you remember the story so well, Taklima. Nobody likes to be hurt or to get bullied. I think Charley must have been really angry about something and forgotten about one of our rules about hitting. Is that right, Charley?

Child nods

TEACHER:   Do you want to say anything to me or to Alex or to any of the children?

CHARLEY:   Alex broke my model and I was cross. I won't hit him again, but he mustn't break my things any more.

Through discussion in a non-punitive environment Charley had the chance to consider both the impact of Alex's behaviour on her and of her actions on him.

*Dress and undress independently and manage their own personal hygiene.*

We do, of course, want children to be independent not only in terms of their learning but in terms of managing their physical needs. With appropriate help and support children learn to dress and undress themselves, wash their hands, use the toilet and feed themselves with little difficulty. Most children will achieve this goal long before the end of the Foundation Stage.

## Summing up

- Children come to your setting with considerable knowledge of their families, themselves, their languages, their culture. It is important to build on this.
- Show respect for the languages, cultures, religions, home backgrounds and family value systems of the children and their families.
- Provide opportunities for children to share, take turns and take part in collaborative play.
- Make sure that children are invited to make choices, follow their own interests and get deeply involved in what it is they are doing.
- Organise your resources and the routines of the day so that children become independent and are able to get involved in doing 'real' jobs for real purposes.
- Be prepared to show what you think is worthwhile. Give clear signals about what you think is good and what not.
- Help children develop an understanding of right and wrong by always giving clear explanations.

- Allow children to express their feelings, even when these are sometimes difficult for you to handle.
- Offer children a cared-for environment and ensure that they don't come across books with pages missing or puzzles with pieces missing.
- Above all, offer a range of meaningful activities so that children can, through first-hand experience, solve problems, communicate with others, express their feelings and understand the social rules.

## Communication, language and literacy

You will know that the development of communication, language and literacy is the key to children's learning. Children need to be able to express their thoughts and ideas in speech and in writing and they need to gain access to the thoughts and ideas of others through listening and reading. Language pervades every activity that children engage in and, since all children are curious, they spend much of their time in the early years trying to understand the symbolic world they encounter. You will remember this from the first chapter of this book.

Two points before we look at the early learning goals. The first is that children learn language and literacy in the same way that they learn about the physical world and the social world. They pay close attention to what those around them are doing and to what they see and hear around them. From this they try to find some pattern which will enable them to work out the rules that apply. Children see print all around them and they begin to wonder what these marks are, why they are there, who made them and why. They begin making marks for themselves and, at the age of about three (although this varies enormously with experience and exposure to print), they begin to describe these marks sometimes as drawing and sometimes as writing. When children are exposed to books and stories they begin to recognise the links between reading and writing: they understand that the marks can be read and that they always say the same thing. So children need to see people around them writing and to have examples of writing to look at. They need to have stories and rhymes read to them and to see competent readers using books. They need time to explore these things for themselves, through play and supported by sensitive interaction. This will foster their learning and understanding far better than instructing children in the letters of the alphabet or the patterns of writing.

The second point is that language does not mean only one language, English. Young children will learn most effectively when they are able to build on what they already know. Children who have a language other than English have already acquired this language. They understand how this language works and are able to use it for thinking. Forcing young children to abandon their first language in order to learn English is both insensitive and damaging. Of course young children do need to learn to speak, read and write in English if they are to succeed in the English school system. The argument is that they will best do this where there own language is valued and respected.

*Interact with others, negotiating plans and activities and taking turns in conversation.*

This early learning goal makes clear the links between speaking and listening and personal, social and emotional development. It also indicates that young children should be in meaningful and often collaborative situations where they have something worth talking about to one another and to the adults. Your setting should be a place where children know that talking to themselves, to one another and to the adults is something that is regarded as worthwhile. There should be opportunities for children to talk about what they are doing, the problems they encounter, the solutions they have come to. Children should be encouraged to talk, but not forced to talk. In schools children sometimes have to endure something called 'news time' where each child is coerced into saying something about what has happened at home over the weekend. This is both socially divisive (what if all that happened to you at the weekend was to listen to your parents arguing or having to help clean up your younger sibling's mess?) and something that young children find difficult to do. Many adults would hate to be put on the spot like that and have to find something to say in front of others.

Ann Browne says:

> Perhaps the most important reason for developing children's oral language is that all learning depends on the ability to question, reason, formulate ideas, pose hypotheses and exchange ideas with others. These are not just oral language skills, they are thinking skills.
>
> (Browne 1996, p. 7)

*Do you agree? Do speaking and listening have a high enough status in your setting?*

*Use talk to organise, sequence and clarify thinking, ideas, feelings and events.*

This early learning goal explicitly recognises the point made by Ann Browne. Good practitioners will be finding ways of helping children develop and refine their skills by making talk an important and valued part of the curriculum. They might invite children to plan aloud what they are going to do; to reflect on what they have done; to share their feelings after a signifi-cant experience; to predict what will happen in practical hands-on activities; to relate stories to events or characters in their own lives; to describe and give reasons; to question and answer.

*Use language to imagine and recreate roles and experiences.*

*Speak clearly and audibly with confidence and control and show awareness of the listener, for example by their use of conventions such as greetings, 'please' and 'thank you'.*

*Extend their vocabulary, exploring the meanings and sounds of new words.*

In settings where talk has a high profile children will be talking as they plan and work. They may talk to themselves, to a friend or in a small group or even, for the most confident children, in a larger group. As they talk they will begin to adjust their tone and register to their audience and this is most successfully developed through role play and drama. Here, where children can take on the roles of others, they can also 'put on' their voices and gestures as they practise being the café manager, the irate mother, the whining baby or the bossy teacher. If you have ever watched a three-year-old playing at being you, you will have been astounded at how much like you this performance is in terms of tone of voice, words used, gestures and body language. Young children are consummate actors as they mimic and exaggerate what they see and hear. As they play and interact they encounter different models of spoken language and in an environment rich with meaningful activities, have opportunities to extend their vocabularies.

*How do you think children's vocabularies might be enhanced in the following play areas? A clinic, a library, a garage, a plant shop? How do you think their vocabularies might be enhanced through visiting the fire station, the corner shop, the local park?*

The rate at which children's vocabulary grows is stunning. When children start in your setting they are usually able to express their needs and desires, to talk about things that are familiar to them and things that matter to them. They have learned all this in their homes and through listening and interaction. Their learning of new words will continue as they are exposed to new and challenging situations and as they encounter new and unfamiliar words in stories read and told.

There used to be the view that adults should use only simple language with young children in order to ensure that they learn new words easily and don't have to cope with difficult words. You will have noticed, however, that very young children are often fascinated by long words – things like stegosaurus, amazing, helicopter. Adults should use normal speech with young children and this can include long words, complex phrases and technical terms. It is important that when adults use mathematical words, like the names of shapes or words of comparison or position, that they use the correct words. Why tell children that bubbles are 'round' when they are, in fact, spherical? Children can learn the word 'sphere' as easily as they can learn the word 'round'.

Children who have had a rich diet of hearing stories read and told will benefit in many ways. One of these is the learning of new words; another is the learning of the very specific language found in books. This 'book language' is different in form and style from the language of speech. You would never say something like 'the road was long and winding and the light became dimmer and dimmer as we walked'. You might say, 'We walked down this long road and it was getting dark'. So the language of books is more complex, more poetic and has its own conventions using phrases like 'Once upon a time' or 'They all lived happily ever after'. Children need to begin to understand this so that when they begin to make up their own stories they are able to use the language of books in their telling and writing.

We all want the children we work with to be regarded as polite and acceptable to the adults they encounter and many of them soon learn the conventional greetings. It is important to remember, however, that there are different ways of greeting and being polite in different cultures. In some cultures it is rude to make eye-to-eye contact. In some cultures thanking is something that is done through the tone of voice. So sensitivity is called for!

*Sustain attentive listening, responding to what they have heard by relevant comments, questions or actions.*

*Listen with enjoyment, and respond to stories, songs and other music, rhymes and poems and make up their own stories, songs, rhymes and poems.*

You will all know how important it is for young children to have as many opportunities to listen and respond to stories, songs, nursery rhymes and poems as possible. In your own setting you will have a wide collection of books in different formats and you will ensure that children can choose to look at and hear books on an individual basis, in a small group or, for the older children, in a large group. Children need to hear new and familiar stories. They need to join in, learning portions or whole texts by heart and they need to have a go at making up their own stories. They need to be allowed to make their own contributions to the story as they hear it in order that they can link it to their own experience. As children get older they are able to listen for longer and longer periods. Most of all we want children to have experienced many different genres and to know that stories, songs, rhymes and poems bring with them other worlds to explore in their heads.

Rainbow Playgroup have organised their wide selection of books so that they have two book corners and other cosy little book 'holes' into which children may crawl, armed with a book or two. This is how they describe their approach to books:

We have many popular children's picture and storybooks, several copies of each, in paperback. We also have some large-format books or Big Books that we use with small groups of children to help them come to understand how books work. We have some information books and some books in English and another language. We don't have enough of those so our aim is to increase the number by the end of this year. We have also made some packs in which we have the book, some story props we have made to go on the magnet board and a tape-recording of the story. With the dual text books we have invited parents in to read the story in the other language. We often use a story as 'a theme' for a few weeks. This term we are using *The Very Hungry Caterpillar*. We have made a wall story and the children made a caterpillar out of old tights stuffed with newspaper and painted. Then we worked out how to make it move by using a pulley. So the caterpillar can crawl through the food and the leaves. The other thing we like to do is to set out a 'small-world' scenario with the books. So with *Mr Gumpy's Outing*, for example, we set up on a table a mirror for the lake, a toy boat, toy animals and Lego people, together with the book. We noticed that many of the children, especially the bilingual children, would play with this for ages, retelling the story or making up their own stories.

The staff at Amandla Early Years Unit have a slightly different agenda:

We are determined to resist pressure to introduce the Literacy Hour too soon because we want the children first and foremost to come to know many books and to know that reading is something pleasurable. We do invite parents to take home a book on a regular basis and often have meetings with parents to show them how we read with the children. The point we want to make is that we want them to read to the children and not test the children's reading.

We do what we call 'Shared Reading' and this is where we use a Big Book with a small group, and when we have read it we sometimes talk to the children about things like punctuation marks, familiar initial sounds (we try and link these to the children's names), directionality of print and so on. We do lots and lots of work around rhyme because we know how children hear rhymes and enjoy playing with them and we all believe that they can do this more successfully than hearing the individual sounds of words.

We also have multiple copies of many of the books and sometimes the children play at schools using these. In the summer term the headteacher wants us to introduce more aspects of the Literacy Hour and we are now planning how to do this in a meaningful way.

*Do you agree with the view that using lots of rhyme is important?*

Children learning to read need, more than anything, to be read to. As they get older they will start to show an interest in aspects of books and of print. They are trying to make sense of the world of print. Some researchers talk about the five aspects or reading:

1  *Literacy awareness*: through exposure to poems, songs, rhymes and stories children's attention can be drawn to things like the direction of the print, the differences and similarities between pictures and print, words and letters. They may see someone point to the words as they read – showing one-to-one correspondence.

2  *Syntactic awareness*: where children have a rich diet of literature they begin to recognise the particular sounds and patterns of the language used in books and, in their own retellings, begin to 'sound like a writer' as they use what is called 'book language'. Many of the books for young children use a highly patterned and repetitive structure that helps the children predict and join in.

3  *Word recognition*: young children quickly learn to recognise their names and those of family members and friends. Good early years practitioners make much of the names of the children, putting them into stories (in, for example, *Mr Gumpy's Outing* where instead of animals, some children go on the boat); making up stories about individual children; writing out the words of songs with children's names in (There was a farmer had a dog and Benny was his name, oh!).

4  *Phonological awareness*: this is the ability to hear and identify sound patterns. There is a considerable body of research evidence (some of this cited by Dombey [1999]) which shows that young children find it difficult to split a spoken word into its component phonemes or sounds. They find it even harder to blend the sounds to make the whole word. They find the initial sound quite easy, the last sound not bad, but the middle sound almost impossible. Because rhyme plays such an important part in the culture of young children, practitioners who use rhyme help children work out words using the initial sound/phoneme (or 'onset') and the rest of the syllable or word (or rime). In the word 'hat', for example, the onset is 'h' and the rime is 'at'. Children find this much simpler than identifying all three phonemes, 'h', 'a', 't'. Goswami (1995) has shown that where children encounter rhymes they can use analogy (spotting patterns) to help them work out new words. So a child who has learned about hat and cat will find 'mat' easy to read. There is also evidence to show that children play with language just as they play with anything else they are trying to make sense of, and in this play rhyming plays a large part. So good early years practitioners will spend a considerable amount of time playing with initial sounds, clapping out the syllables and making up rhymes. Many of the skipping, clapping songs help children identify and pay attention to syllables. Young

children also enjoy making up alliterative sentences – sentences where each word starts with the same letter (exciting Ellie eats elephants: brave Bilal bites bananas).

5 *Orthographic awareness*: this involves labelling the letters of the alphabet and is something that many parents are keen to see their children do. Children enjoy chanting the alphabet and may look at alphabet friezes. They may pay attention to the letter at the start of their name and enjoy playing with magnetic letters.

It needs to be re-emphasised that all of this needs to take place in the context of story and play. Decontextualised activities like flashcards and worksheets will not foster children's learning and development. Although the children may show short-term gains, do remember the work of Katz and Elkind referred to in Chapter 1 which shows how such gains often represent long-term damage to the disposition to learn.

When you look at the following early learning goals you will want to keep in mind what you have just read and remember that, in helping children become readers, familiarity with a range of written forms, play with rhyme, alliteration and syllable, knowledge of the alphabet and opportunities to make analogies and talk about their findings will be more helpful than simple decoding practice.

*Explore and experiment with sounds, words and texts.*

*Know that print carries meaning and, in English, is read from left to right and top to bottom.*

*Hear and say initial and final sounds in words and short vowel sounds within words.*

*Link sounds to letters, naming and sounding the letters of the alphabet.*

In terms of helping children make up their own stories, songs and rhymes it is primarily through role play that children invent scenarios and characters. Practitioners who are skilled storytellers use different voices and props and sometimes let the children take charge of how the story develops. They know that children who have a story told and read are fortunate in coming to understand that it is the print in the book version that makes the story exactly the same each time it is read. In terms of becoming a reader this is an important lesson to learn.

Let us turn our attention to more of the early learning goals concerned primarily with emergent reading and consider what provision we can make to foster this.

*Retell narratives in the correct sequence, drawing on language patterns of stories.*

*Show an understanding of the elements of stories, such as main character, sequence of events, and openings and how information can be found in non-fiction texts to answer questions about where, who, why and how.*

Hannah, aged four, talked about stories with happy endings and reflected that in all those she had come across there was a bad character. Her developing understanding of the conventions of stories led her to consider good overcoming evil.

'This is a book written by Roald Dahl, with pictures by Quentin Blake', the adult said. The child, aged five, asked, ' Don't you mean "illustrated by Quentin Blake?"'

Sukvinder, aged three, tells her mum the story of 'Goldilocks and the Three Bears': 'Daddy Bear, Mummy Bear and Baby Bear and a little girl came and she ate the porridge and she broke the chair and she went to bed and she went home and that's the end.'

Ben wants someone to read him the instructions that came with a set of magnets. 'Do they tell you how they work?'

What can we do?

- Provide information books for children to explore.
- Read recipes, planting instructions, etc. in context, aloud to the children.
- Talk to children about books – not only about details like 'front' and 'back' and 'cover', but also talk to them about the sometimes deep and difficult themes in books. *Not Now, Bernard* is about a child being ignored by his parents: *Mine* is about jealousy: talk to children about the main characters and invite them to talk about what these characters are like.
- Welcome children's popular culture (television, film, video, pop music) into the classroom and use these as themes to promote literacy.

And finally, in terms of reading, you might want to think carefully about how to provide learning opportunities to help children achieve this goal.

*Read a range of familiar and common words and simple sentences independently.*

There is no doubt that some children will have had enough experience of activities associated with speaking and listening, reading and writing to be able to read by the time they leave the reception class. Children who have been immersed in stories and book language and who have played with alliteration and rhyme find reading immensely rewarding and go on to be readers. But there are many children who still fear that reading is difficult and that they will fail. Approaches to reading which 'test' children often result in fear of failure. Confidence, self-esteem and enjoyment are pre-requisites for becoming readers.

Do remember that writers of good books for children play with language in ways that help children read. What is more this is done in the context of something that is exciting or funny or sad. First of all the children are drawn into the story and then they are drawn into the text. And as they hear the story again and again they are able to join in and predict and, eventually, to read.

Consider these sentences, taken from some children's books

My old Teddy's leg came off. Poor old Teddy!
I took him to the Teddy doctor. She made Teddy better.
My old Teddy's leg came off. Poor old Teddy.
I took him to the Teddy doctor. She made Teddy better.
(D. Mansell, My Old Teddy)

Here's a little baby
One, two, three
Stands in his cot
What does he see?
(Janet and Allen Ahlberg, Peepo)

. . . Auntie, Auntie Bibba.
Auntie Bibba came inside with her
Arms wide, wide, wide
And one big, big smile.
'Oooh!' she said.
'I want to squeeze him,
I want to squeeze the baby,
I want to squeeze him
SO MUCH!'
(Trish Cooke, So Much)

You don't have here the wonderful pictures that extend and enhance the texts, but even from these brief extracts you can see the devices used by good authors: humour, repetition, rhythm, rhyme, using children's experience and interests. Immersion in books like these, together with talk about authors and illustrators, characters and words, will make reading possible and satisfying for all children.

We will now look at children exploring mark-making and writing and turn our attention to the early learning goals focused on this aspect of communication, language and literacy.

*Enjoy listening to and using spoken and written language, and readily turn to it in their play and learning.*

*Attempt writing for different purposes, using features of different forms such as lists, stories and instructions.*

Young children begin to write as part of their exploration of their physical world. Making marks with a finger on a misted window pane or with a stick in the sand, children begin to realise that their hands themselves, or a tool used as an extension of their hands, can leave a trace. Once children are offered pencils or crayons they discover that the marks they make are permanent. This is a satisfying event and one children are keen to repeat – often with disastrous consequences on walls and floors! Children's earliest marks are not representations of anything, but a record of their physical movements. But as children see people around them engaged in writing they begin to want to discover what it is that these people are doing. So their own mark-making becomes more intentional and the intention is often to communicate some meaning.

When children enter your setting they are often able to say that their marks are either drawings or writing. In other words they recognise the differences between two symbolic systems – a significant achievement in itself! In their earliest attempts at writing they will often include writing-like patterns and letter-like shapes. Do remember that children who have seen adults using Bengali script, for example, will include Bengali letter-like shapes in their writing. This, again, is evidence of children's knowledge and not of their lack of knowledge. As children see more modelling of writing and as they see writing in books, in the setting and in the world around them, their attempts at writing will move closer and closer to recognisable letters. Often the first letters you will recognise will be the letters in the child's name. It is worth paying close attention to what it is the children are doing as they write and it is important to remember that writing is more difficult than reading since it involves the skills of actually forming the letters, words and sentences as well as making up the meaning.

Children are not only working out how the written system works, but also trying to understand the different functions and purposes for writing. They see adults around them engaged in acts of writing for different purposes – a note to the milkman, an entry in a diary, a message on the message board, a letter to Gran, a form in the post office and so on. In your setting you should try to offer children opportunities to explore the purposes of writing in as many meaningful ways as possible.

Here, again, is what Rainbow Playgroup decided to do to encourage children to explore the purposes of writing:

> Well, first we set up a writing corner. We put up alphabet charts in three languages (English, Bengali and Turkish). We put in an old typewriter, a stapler, a hole punch, scissors, lots of different sizes and types of pencils, crayons, coloured pencils, felt pens. We put out small books of blank pages stapled together, writing paper, strips of paper, envelopes, blank forms. The children often go in there and do their own writing. We notice that they always write in the boxes of the blank forms! We time-table ourselves so that one of us is always in the writing corner, some-times writing our letters or shopping lists. The children are always interested in what we are doing and want to have a go themselves.
>
> We try and think of what examples of, and opportunities for, writing we can put in our imaginative play areas. Last term we had a café and the children helped us make signs for the café. We wrote up a menu and there were little notebooks for the children to use when they took an order. There were strips of paper for them to use for the bills. One member of staff brought in an old cheque book and the children had a great time writing cheques! One of the children suggested we had a recipe book so the cook would know what to cook and so the children made their own recipe book which included pictures and their attempts at writing or our writing when they wanted us to write for them.

The Amandla Early Years Unit visited Rainbow Playgroup to look at their provision and added the following ideas, thinking particularly about pro-viding for the learning needs of the children in the reception classes:

> We read Nigel Hall's work about play and literacy and decided to set up a garage in the classroom. We visited a garage and the children helped us decide how to set it up, what notices to write and then we intervened. We told the children that if they wanted to play in the garage they had to apply and that led to a discussion about what it meant to apply. Drawing on Hall's work we worked with the children to devise a job advert and a job description and the children then filled in the forms we designed. The forms had information required like child's name, address, phone number, plus a space to write 'Why you would be good at this job'. Children all enjoyed designing the adverts and forms and filled them in well, giving us an idea of what they could write unaided.

*Write their own names and other things such as labels and captions and begin to form simple sentences, sometimes using punctuation.*

*Use their phonic knowledge to write simple regular words and make phonetically plausible attempts at more complex words.*

*Use a pencil and hold it effectively to form recognisable letters, most of which are correctly formed.*

In order to plan for and promote early writing it is important to understand something about what is known about how young children make sense of print as they attempt to do it for themselves. Writing is a complex thing: it involves both deciding what to write (which is called composition) and knowing how to make the relevant marks on paper (which is called transcription). Transcription involves children knowing something about how to form the letters (what we call 'handwriting') and how to spell the actual words and put them down on the paper. So it involves working out the rules of spelling and of grammar (things like capital letters, punctuation, spaces between words). You may have children come and ask you to write something for them – e.g. 'write "I love you, Mummy" or "Come to my house to play".' And you may have seen children making marks on paper that they call writing (as opposed to drawing) and revealing their developing concepts about the written system. A child may move from strings of letter-like shapes to rows of letters (often drawn from their names) to words made up of initial and last sound (I LV U) to some correctly spelled words combined with abbreviated forms. Children experiment with capital and lower-case letters and often incorporate punctuation marks in their writing.

As with all other aspects of learning children see experienced writers writing and they see writing in the environment – on television, products, in books and magazines, etc. They have a go at making similar marks for themselves and later say that these marks 'say something'. There are many books and articles about this early writing, and we don't have room in this book to go into this in any detail. It is important, though, that children have opportunities for writing, that they see others writing, that they are encouraged to have a go and that, as they get older and more aware of the relationships between letters, sounds and words, they don't lose the confidence to try for themselves.

## Summing it up

- Language pervades every area of learning.
- Children learn language and literacy as active learners trying to understand the world they inhabit.
- Children who have already acquired a language other than English should be supported in using this language as they acquire English.
- A good nursery or playgroup is one where children and adults know that talking is respected and valued.

- Adults should use appropriate language which is aimed to help children understand and to move on in their learning.
- Books introduce children to wider worlds and increased vocabulary as well as the very specific language of books.
- All young children should have access to books, rhymes, songs and stories on a regular basis individually and in small groups.
- Children should have opportunities to retell known stories and to make up their own stories. Adults should try telling stories as well as reading them.
- Adults should help children come to understand how books work by drawing their attention to the direction of print, inviting them to turn pages, helping them focus on the print itself and begin to realise that it is people who write and illustrate books.
- Adults can help children find the patterns in language by spending some considerable time reading and creating rhymes, singing songs and encouraging children to play with spoken and written language.
- Adults should, above all, help children realise that, in reading, the task is to lift the writer's meaning from the page. They should help children use all means available to them to understand and then retell the story.
- Adults can introduce children to many aspects of literacy by including children's names in stories, songs, rhymes and games. Children's names are significant to them and using them offers many opportunities for children to learn about letters and sounds.
- Adults should display alphabets and scripts in the languages of the children and should offer children magnetic letters to play with.
- Adults should ensure that they provide many opportunities for children to explore reading and writing through familiar and meaningful situations.
- Adults should model both reading and writing, showing children how expert readers and writers operate.
- Adults should pay close attention to what the children do as they play at reading and writing and use this to inform their planning.
- Adults need to remember that writing is a complex skill and be willing to 'scribe' for the children.

## References

Browne, A. (1996) *Developing Language and Literacy 3–8*, London, PCP.
DfEE (1998) *The National Literacy Strategy*, London, HMSO.
DfEE and QCA (2000) *Curriculum Guidance for the Foundation Stage*, London, QCA.
DfEE and QCA (2000) *Curriculum Guidance for the Foundation Stage*, London, DfEE.
Dombey, H. (1999) 'Questioning Phonics', *Literacy Today*, no. 20, September.
Dunn, J. (1988) *The Beginnings of Social Understanding*, Oxford, Basil Blackwell.

Goswami, U. (1995) 'Phonological development and reading by analogy: what is analogy and what is it not?' *Journal of Research in Reading* 18(2), 139–45.

Gregory, E. (1996) *Making Sense of a New World: Learning to Read in a Second Language*, London, PCP.

Hall, N. (1999) 'Young Children, Play and Literacy: Engagement in Realistic Uses of Literacy', in J. Marsh and E. Hallet (eds), *Desirable Literacies*, London, PCP.

Heath, S.B. (1983) *Ways with Words: Language, Life and Work in Communities and Classrooms*, Cambridge, Cambridge University Press.

Katz, L. (1988) 'What Should Young Children Be Doing?', *American Educator*, Summer.

Marsh, J. and Hallet, E. (eds) (1999) *Desirable Literacies*, London, PCP.

Smith, M. (1998) 'Making Honey', in S. Smidt (ed.), *The Early Years: A Reader*, London, Routledge.

Trevarthen, C. (1998) 'The Child's Need to Learn a Culture', in M. Woodhead, D. Faulkner and K. Littleton (eds), *Cultural Worlds of Early Childhood*, London, Routledge.

Voss, B. (1998) 'Supporting Young Children', in S. Smidt (ed.), *The Early Years: A Reader*, London, Routledge.

Woodhead, M., Faulkner, D. and Littleton, K. (eds) (1998) *Cultural Worlds of Early Childhood*, London, Routledge.

### Children's texts

Ahlberg, J. and A. (1981) *Peepo*, London, Puffin.

Cooke, T. (1994) *So Much*, London, Walker Books.

Mansell, D. (1993) *My Old Teddy*, London, Walker Books.

# Chapter 5

# Understanding and explaining the physical world

Dov (aged four) arrives at the playgroup and hangs his coat on his peg. He then goes over to the book corner and spends about twenty minutes sorting out the books in one of the book boxes. An adult (who has decided to observe Dov for that morning) notices that he is making piles of books of the same size. Satisfied with that he goes over to the junk modelling area and sorts out some things he wants to use. He selects an empty box and a yoghurt carton, together with some brightly coloured wrapping paper. He spends the next hour or so attempting to wrap up his chosen boxes. He manages to wrap the box by placing it in the centre of a large piece of paper and folding the paper so that the entire box is hidden. He fastens the paper down using sellotape. The yoghurt carton causes him more difficulty. He attempts to cover it in the same way as the box, but the shape is difficult for him to manage. The worker notices that he keeps picking up the yoghurt carton and examining it and each time he does this he cuts the wrapping paper. Observing that he will not be successful in this chosen task the worker offers him help, which he accepts. Happy with his wrapped boxes he joins three girls in the construction area and watches what they are doing. He then carefully selects some blocks and proceeds to build a wall. In doing this the worker notices that he starts off using blocks of the same length, but when he runs out of those on the second layer of his wall he resorts to using two smaller blocks, which are equivalent to one large block. At tidying-up time he joins the girls in carefully stacking the blocks in the correct place. The stencils of the shapes of the blocks placed on the shelves help him to match them. In his story group he happily joins in with the songs, and the worker notices that when they are singing counting songs Dov is using his fingers to count on. It is Dov's turn to set the tables for lunch and he is very efficient at setting the table for five children and one adult.

*What do you think the worker wrote down about what Dov knows about mathematics?*

Dov, like most children of his age, has already learned a great deal about counting, matching, sorting, estimating, shape and space, patterns and solving problems. He has learned much of this at home in the everyday activities which involve mathematics. Here is what Dov's keyworker wrote in her analysis of what he knew:

> Dov can sort and match according to size and shape. He is able to estimate area and used his eye to check on the size of the box and the size of the paper. He understands that two smaller blocks are equal in length to one long block. He knows a lot of number songs and uses his fingers to count on. He understands about one-to-one correspondence and was able to set the table with one fork, one knife, one spoon, one table mat and one cup for each person. He also knew that the adult setting used larger utensils.

Mathematics is a word that strikes terror in the hearts of many childcare and nursery practitioners and even in the hearts of many teachers, who are having to upgrade their own mathematical knowledge in order to be recognised as teachers. Yet we use mathematics all the time in our everyday lives. What is interesting is that we are often unaware that we are using mathematics.

*Write down all the things you have done this week which involved mathematics.*
Did you come up with any of these things?

✓ put up shelves
✓ made sure you were on the correct bus
✓ worked out how much time you needed to make a journey
✓ put a casserole in the oven for an hour and twenty minutes
✓ checked you had been given the correct change
✓ measured your child
✓ wrapped a parcel
✓ followed a knitting pattern
✓ cut a slice of bread in half.

We are all able to do these things without difficulty, just as we are able to pick up a pencil or turn on the TV. Yet all of them involve the skills and knowledge we call mathematics.

In the Foundation Stage mathematical knowledge has a high priority. What is emphasised is children enjoying mathematical knowledge because it is purposeful; children being confident and able not only to solve problems but know how they did so; and children being able to use mathematical language in their play. Practitioners have a vital role to play in this and practitioners who themselves become confident about their own knowledge of mathematics will engender confidence and enjoyment in the children.

In line with the *National Numeracy Strategy: Framework for Teaching* the focus moves from the detail found in the earlier 'Desirable Outcomes' to broader areas, including finding out about and using numbers, calculation, pattern, shape, space and measures. Just as in all other areas of learning in the Foundation Stage children should be involved in first-hand practical experience in meaningful contexts. The adults working with them should strive to use the correct mathematical language to help children use this very specific language themselves to describe and explain the processes they are involved in.

Mathematics is an area of learning which is not necessarily dependent on understanding and speaking English. In lifelike contexts, where the meaning is embedded in the activity, children who have English as an additional language will be able to engage in problem-solving activities alongside their English-speaking peers. This is only true if the children can see the purpose of any activity or select to use the materials on offer in a way which meets their needs and interests.

There are four early learning goals that relate to using numbers as labels and for counting. These are:

*Say and use number names in order in familiar contexts.*

*Count reliably up to ten everyday objects.*

*Recognise numerals 1 to 9.*

*Use developing mathematical ideas and methods to solve practical problems.*

Most young children use number names in their everyday conversation. They talk about their age, attempt to count, memorise number songs and certainly understand small numbers when it comes to getting something nice – like sweets or cakes. With experience, their understanding of numbers increases and their use of number names becomes more accurate. Similarly, children start counting objects in their play, often inaccurately at first. Again, with support and experience they become more accurate.

Just as you would ensure that you have alphabets displayed in your room so you would want to have a number line and, if at all possible, a number line for the number symbols in other languages. You would also want to ensure that you have magnetic numerals and numbers displayed where relevant and appropriate. Children see numerals around them – on buses, on television, on their front doors and in shops. They are often interested to know what these say and will even include numerals in their mark-making.

Some numbers are significant to children and the most obvious ones relate to their ages. Pat Gura (1996) gives a lovely example of three-year-old Sean exploring how to represent his exact age of three and a half. In a group of children aged three to six who were talking about their ages and examining a set of numerals, Sean selected the numeral '3' and placed it on the magnet board:

> ADULT: 'Three. That's good. Now what about the half? Shall I show you how to do that?' (Sean nods. Andrew and Joshua move closer.) Next to Sean's three, the adult creates the symbol for 'half' with three pieces: 'There you are, Sean. Now it says three and a half.'
> Sean is very pleased but Joshua is enthralled. He promptly copies the three and a half, telling anyone who cares to listen: 'That says three and a half'. Then, announcing each one as he goes along, he makes four and a half, eight and a half, nought and a half, nine and a half, two and a half. At this point he stops and reads them all back.
>
> (Gura 1996, p. 150)

It is interesting to note that children in the Foundation Stage are not required to record numbers. An understanding of how numbers work and the ability to recognise the symbols is what matters. You might want to consider what this example of a five-year-old girl tells you about how a particular interest can lead children to achieve a lot more than is expected in the early learning goals.

> In her play Hannah decided to make a measuring chart. She got four pieces of paper and stuck them together. She then started at the bottom of the page with number one and went up the page creating a totally accurate number line. She wrote the numbers correctly up to 137 and then went on to measure herself, her brother, her best friend, two dolls and a toy lion.

Those working with young children will use number songs, rhymes, stories and games as part of their daily provision. Most children coming to your setting will already know some number songs and rhymes. These may be in English or in the languages spoken at home. Young children greatly enjoy singing such songs and chanting rhymes, particularly when they are brought to life either through using props on a magnet board or a felt board, or by using the children themselves. It is worth building up your collection of number rhymes and songs and inviting parents and carers to teach you songs and rhymes you don't yet know and which may be in the languages spoken by the children. And you may want to record these on to tapes so that the children can choose to listen to them when you are not available to sing them. Making Big Books of these songs and rhymes provides an invaluable resource and brings to life the links between literacy and mathematics.

*How many of these songs and rhymes do you know?*

One, two, three, four, five
Once I caught a fish alive . . .

One, two, buckle my shoe . . .

Two, four, six, eight,
Mary at the garden gate . . .

Five elephants went out to play
On a spider's web one day . . .

Five currant buns in the baker's shop . . .

Five little speckled frogs sat on a speckled log . . .

There were six little frogs
Sitting on a well . . .

When Goldilocks went to the house of the bears
Oh what did her blue eyes see? . . .

Five little monkeys jumping on the bed
One fell off and banged his head . . .

Stories are another invaluable source for mathematical ideas and concepts. If you take the time to look through some of the books and stories you know well you will find mathematics embedded in the stories. There are many attractive counting books and children may well be interested in these, and you should certainly ensure that you have some. But just as reading is about more than simply decoding the words, understanding mathematical concepts comes more through exploring these concepts in situations that children understand than through merely chanting them.

*Here are some excellent children's books to consider. Take the time to look at each and see if you can identify what aspects of mathematics are explored through both text and pictures.*

*Where's Spot?*
*Titch*
*The Three Billy Goats Gruff*
*What's the Time, Mr. Wolf?*
*Mr Gumpy's Outing.*

*How did you get on with this task?*

Finally, in this section, it is worth thinking about stories you can make up to explore different mathematical concepts. In doing this you should also think of what props you can introduce so that in the telling of your story you give the children physical support for the concepts. Hilary Faust, an early years mathematics consultant has made up many such stories and she insists that, after the telling of the story, the props be left out for the children to play with as they retell the story or create their own story. One of her stories concerns a teddy bear who decides to send his cousin a birthday present. He finds a small bowl (which Hilary shows to the children) and then looks for a box to put the bowl in. Hilary has a collection of boxes, some of which are too small and some of which are too big. There is only one which is 'just right'.

Games are another way of helping children understand number concepts. There are many commercially produced games and you will want to examine them to ensure that they will be relevant and meaningful to the children and that they do not reflect images which are monocultural or even offensive. There are also the traditional games of hopscotch, skipping games, finger plays, circle games and ball/bat/hoop games. In these, the players (including the adults) share the agreed rules and can only change them by negotiating.

You can also make games, and when you do you can ensure that they meet the learning needs you have identified from your observations of the children. Some of the best games derive from the stories you read. Here is an example to illustrate this:

> Jenny, one of the nursery nurses in a reception class, noticed that some of the children were interested in large numbers. She decided to make a game based on a popular picture book, *Not Now, Bernard*. The game was essentially a number line and the children had to throw the dice and move the number of steps indicated by the number on the dice. The number line moved from Bernard being ignored by his parents to the monster ending up in Bernard's bed and the number line went from 1 to 100.

The children played the game with enthusiasm, initially always with an adult present, but later on they were able to play on their own. After a few weeks Jenny decided that the children might need some cognitive challenge and so she added some labels to the number line in the form of pictures of the monster roaring. Each time the child landed on one of these pictures she or he had to go backwards rather than forwards, each time the number of steps indicated on the dice. In this way she was helping the children explore both counting on and counting down.

This proves as a good introduction to the early learning goals connected with calculating. These are:

*In practical activities and discussion begin to use the vocabulary involved in adding and subtracting.*

*Use language such as 'more' and 'less' to compare two numbers.*

*Find one more or one less than a number from one to ten.*

*Begin to relate addition to combining two groups of objects and subtraction to 'taking away'.*

Through practical activities, games, songs, rhymes, stories and discussion children start exploring what happens when things are added to or taken away from something. Many children have experience of this in their real lives, as when they ask for 'one more' or when Mum says, 'If you don't share I will take it away'. Here are some examples:

Rosie and Shameela in the home corner, setting the table. Rosie counts out the chairs: 'One, two, three, four'. She counts the dolls: 'One, two, three'. Then she says to Shameela: 'Get another chair, Sham. We need five and there's only four here.'

Anneka and Liam are setting the table for lunch. Liam puts out seven place mats and Anneka tells him to take one away because there are only six children at that table.

Zubeida says: 'If you give me one more I will have more than Tommy.'

Paulina and Dean are playing a game using dice. Pauline throws a three and then a two.
'Three and two: that makes five, so I can move five places.' The nursery nurse asked: 'How did you work that out, Paulina. Did you start with three and count on like this?'

Abi, Darren and Charlotte are handing out slices of orange at circle time. Charlotte turns to the adult and says: 'I need two more pieces for me and Morwen.'

During a singing session six children are at the front, pretending to be frogs. Bobby suddenly shouts out: 'If Marcus and Valya sit down there will be four left.' The teacher asked, 'How did you work that out, Bobby?' And Bobby replied, 'I counted six on my fingers and then put two fingers down and I had four left.'

The role of the adult in all of this is to use the correct mathematical language with the children; to pose problems when reading stories or chanting songs; to show an interest in how the children arrived at an answer or a solution; and provide opportunities for games and opportunities for addition and subtraction in role-play areas.

We come now to the early learning goals related to pattern, shape, space and measures. As you read through them please notice the emphasis placed on the language of mathematics.

*Talk about, recognise and recreate simple patterns.*

*Use language such as 'circle' or 'bigger' to describe the shape and size of solids and flat shapes.*

*Use everyday words to describe position.*

If I asked you to tell me some 'mathematical terms', I imagine you would come up with words like 'circle', 'square', 'big', 'small', 'more', 'less' and 'equals'. The language of mathematics includes words relating to everyday life and you may be surprised to discover just how many of them you use without even realising this. You will discover more about this in the section about physical development.

*You might like to read through the next example and underline the words which could be described as 'mathematical':*

Three children are playing on the outdoor climbing frame.

SUNITA:   I'm climbing right to the top. I am higher than you.
SORAYA:   I can climb even higher. See, I'm the very highest.
PRIYA:    I am coming next to you then I'll also be the very highest.
SUNITA:   Let's go across here. You can follow me. I am going first and then you, Priya and you last [points to Soraya]. Then we can go underneath and hang down.

Here are some of the words underlined by a group of teachers and childcare practitioners in a workshop: top, higher, highest, next to, across, first, last, underneath, down. *Did any of those words surprise you?*

The children, in their play, were using mathematical language to describe their comparisons of height and also to explore position and direction.

Some practitioners, on reading this outcome, may try to teach children mathematical terms through decontextualised activities – like asking children to colour all the circles on a worksheet red and all the triangles blue. Compare this type of activity which involves the child in merely follow-ing instructions with a self-chosen activity where the child is involved in physically exploring the properties of shapes – as in painting, drawing, select-ing materials to make a model.

Piaget talks of two different types of knowledge that children use when they act on objects. He called these 'physical knowledge' (which relates to what children discover about objects they handle) and 'logicomathematical knowledge' (which relates to what children discover when they make com-parisons between objects). For Piaget physical knowledge comes from infor-mation external to the child – from the direct physical exploration of the objects. The source of logicomathematical knowledge is internal: it is what happens inside the child's head. It is important to note that, for Piaget, the two are intertwined and the child cannot separate out one type of knowledge from another. A child comes to recognise the colour red by comparing objects of different colours and by classifying them. No child is able to classify objects without a great deal of experience of exploring them using both his or her senses and physical exploration of objects. The children on the climbing frame in the example above are physically exploring space and position and have obviously explored these concepts before. Through their physical and sensory explorations they have come to understand the concepts of higher and highest.

In order for children to develop the language of mathematics they need to explore the physical properties of objects in order to classify, sort, match, sequence and count. It is only through doing this in situations that are personally meaningful to them that they are able to internalise the concepts so that they are later able to use this language with understanding

Here are some contexts set up in nurseries, playgroups and reception classes which offer opportunities for a number of aspects of mathematical exploration and the use of mathematical language. *In each one you might like to decide what aspects of mathematics the children are invited to explore and how the adults involved have ensured this in their planning and provision*:

> The children are baking cookies. Each child has a bowl and a spoon and the adult has written the recipe out in large script and reads it aloud as she helps the children in the process. There are six children in the group and the adult has a cookie tin with twelve sections.

> The class has read the story 'The Three Bears' and the staff have re-arranged the home corner so that is has become the bears' cottage. In the home corner are three chairs of different sizes, three beds of different sizes and three bowls of different sizes.

> All the children take turns to help set the tables for lunch each day. They have to set a place for each of six children and an additional place for the

adult. Each place has a knife, a fork, a spoon and a glass. The children's utensils are smaller than those for the adult.

In the garden the staff have set up a bus station and have put a number on each of the cars and trikes.

The theme in the reception class is the story of 'Jack and the Beanstalk'. The home corner has been turned into the Giant's castle and contains a giant bowl and a giant spoon. The beanstalk goes from floor to ceiling.

One of the things that young children do as they come to understand the world is to try and find the patterns they encounter. These can be the patterns relating to language, as we saw in an earlier chapter, or the patterns they see in tiles or wallpaper or in mathematics.

Mathematics, which is a symbolic way of explaining and describing aspects of the physical world, is highly dependent on pattern and on rules. We classify and sort things according to what features they have in common. A child playing with six wooden blocks – four red and two blue, for example – might sort them according to colour or might line them up in a pattern – two red, one blue, two red, one blue – or might even just divide them into two equal piles. As in all early learning, young children need to see patterns in their world and to create and recreate them according to their own interests.

Here are two examples. *In each case consider what you think the child is learning about pattern and rules:*

The children are at a table threading beads. Each child has been given a card which shows a pattern of beads and has been asked to copy that pattern.

Four children in the block play area have constructed a 'building' and have used cylindrical blocks separated out by small cubes. The adult watching them comments, 'I like the pattern you have used – cylinder, cube, cylinder, cube.'

The last early learning goal for this learning area is:

*Use developing mathematical ideas and methods to solve practical problems.*

Young children in your setting will already be using their developing mathematical understanding to solve practical problems. You have only to observe children playing in the home corner or the outdoor play space or the construction or creative areas to notice how often they do this. Reread the example of Dov at the beginning of this chapter to see just how many practical problems Dov solves in his play.

Greco (1962) gives a fascinating example of just how important it is to let children actually solve problems for themselves rather than giving them 'fake' problems to solve. How many of you, I wonder, can still remember some of the meaningless mathematical problems you encountered at school: problems of the type 'If John has seventeen liquorice sticks and twelve sherbet lemons and his sister has twice as many liquorice sticks and half the number of sherbet lemons, how many sweets does his sister have?' Greco's example concerned a five-year-old boy called Jean-Pierre who lived with his mother, father and sibling:

> Jean-Pierre could count to 30. Each day his mother asked him to put out the table napkins for the main meal of the day. On the first day Jean-Pierre took out one napkin and put it on one plate. He then returned to the cupboard in order to get the second napkin which he put on the second plate. In all he made four trips in order to match each napkin to each plate. About three months later he decided to count the plates and then counted out four napkins. This continued for six days.
>
> On the seventh day there was a guest for dinner and Jean-Pierre found an additional plate on the table. He took out four napkins as usual, but then realised that there was a plate without a napkin. Dismayed by this he returned all four napkins to the cupboard and started all over again, this time making five trips to and from the table.
>
> The next day the guest was no longer there, but Jean-Pierre made four trips to the table and he kept up this method for five more days, when he returned to his previous method of counting plates and counting napkins. Ten days later he was told that there was to be a guest for dinner again. This time he counted out his four napkins and then returned to the cupboard to get an extra one for the guest. And on the following day when it was only the family for dinner he calmly counted out four plates and four napkins. The presence of guests for dinner never again disturbed his counting system.
>
> (Greco 1962, cited in Williams and Kamii 1986, p. 25)

## Summing it up

- Children learn about mathematical concepts through their everyday experiences as they try to understand the world in which they live.
- Children entering your setting have already learned a great deal about counting, matching, sorting, classifying, ordering, comparing and sequencing. They have also learned about pattern, shape, space and measures.

- Mathematics is embedded in most of the activities of everyday life. Practitioners should try to be more alert to the mathematical potential of everyday activities.
- Children who have a language other than English can explore mathematical concepts without being dependent on understanding or speaking English.
- Children should encounter numerous opportunities to explore objects and to be involved in first-hand experience. This will allow them to move to the stage where they are no longer dependent on handling objects because they can hold concepts in their heads.
- The use of mathematical language is an important part of development. Children should be helped by adults to acquire the specific language of mathematics and adults should listen attentively to children to discover just how much they understand.
- Adults should show a genuine interest in how children have solved problems.
- Offering children opportunities to explore mathematical concepts in meaningful situations will help children both build on what they already know and move ahead in their learning.
- Songs, rhymes, games and stories provide an invaluable resource for the development of mathematical concepts and language.
- Opportunities should be provided for children to explore shape, space and pattern.
- Numerals should be displayed and children invited to examine and explore these.
- Just as names are significant to children, so are ages. Practitioners should explore possibilities for building on children's interest in their ages (and sometimes those of their friends and family members).
- Practitioners should offer children opportunities to think and to solve problems, rather than giving them recipes or solutions. In this way children are allowed to be inventive, thoughtful and to develop confidence in their own abilities to solve problems they encounter in their play and learning.

## Physical development

You will remember, from the first chapter of this book, how the human brain requires oxygen and you will know, from your own experience, how young children really need to be physically active as they learn and play. One of the most damaging features of children starting formal schooling very young is that they are required to be seated, often indoors, for long periods of time. The Foundation Stage now offers those working with children in the reception class the justification for finding ways for these children, in parallel with younger children in all settings, to have ongoing access to

some outdoor area where they are able to develop the skills of running, jumping, balancing, climbing, riding small vehicles, pushing, pulling, catching,
throwing, sliding and so on. Young children's physical skills develop rapidly
and they enjoy their developing prowess which gives them greater and greater
control over their environment. Children's fine motor skills also develop
rapidly, particularly where children are given free access to a range of tools,
objects, construction materials and malleable materials to explore.

Practitioners should plan activities that offer physical challenges, that are
imaginative and enjoyable and they should allow children the time and the
space in which to develop their skills. It is important to remind ourselves
of the fact that the more varied experiences children have to explore the
physical world the more neural connections are laid down. In other words,
the more attention you pay to what you provide for children to use and
explore, the greater the opportunity for children to learn.

The early learning goals focus on various aspects of physical development:
movement; sense of space; health and bodily awareness; use of tools, materials
and equipment.

There are three early learning goals related to developing movement:

*Move with confidence, imagination and in safety.*

*Move with control and coordination.*

*Travel around, under, over and through balancing and climbing equipment.*

*Do you think that you have to plan for physical development or is it enough just to
make sure that the climbing frame, the hoops and ropes and the balance beams are in
place?*

If you want children to grow in confidence and to refine their skills you
need to plan for progression in physical development just as you do for
other areas of learning. This means that you need to plan what you will
make available in the outdoor play area each day. It is important to remember
not to offer the same activities and materials day in and day out. If you do this
you remove the possibility for children to develop increasing control and
awareness. Do remember the theory of 'Match' mentioned in an earlier
chapter, which suggests that something new should be added to or removed
from a situation in order to take learning forward, but that this change should
be carefully matched to the child's interests and needs.

Here are some examples to illustrate this:

A worker at the Rainbow Playgroup noticed that four-year-old Tamina,
who was very small for her age, was finding it difficult to join her friends
in playing on the climbing frame because she found the height of the first
step daunting. The worker placed a wooden block at the base of the steps.

She observed what happened and was intrigued to find that, not only did this block achieve her aim of giving Tamina the confidence to climb up the steps, but that the other children used the block as something to leap over when they came down the steps!

The staff at a playgroup working in a church hall with no access to outdoor space set up 'A' frames with planks in order to ensure the children have some opportunity every day to develop some physical skills. Using only two 'A' frames and three planks of wood they are able to vary the layout so that children are offered 'bridges' to walk across, ramps to climb up and slide down and enclosed areas to explore. The addition of objects like blankets, torches, picnic baskets, a steering wheel and some milk crates allow the children to turn the 'A' frames into different environments to explore.

The coordinator of Amandla Early Years Unit asked her staff to plan what aspects of physical development would be catered for each week. This involved the staff in much discussion about what physical activities the children needed to acquire or refine and what materials and resources they should offer. One planning sheet looked like that shown in Figure 5.1.

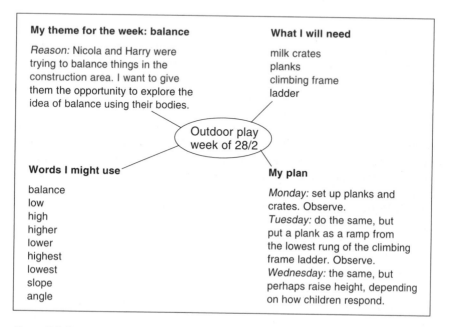

**My theme for the week: balance**

*Reason:* Nicola and Harry were trying to balance things in the construction area. I want to give them the opportunity to explore the idea of balance using their bodies.

**What I will need**

milk crates
planks
climbing frame
ladder

Outdoor play week of 28/2

**Words I might use**

balance
low
high
higher
lower
highest
lowest
slope
angle

**My plan**

*Monday:* set up planks and crates. Observe.
*Tuesday:* do the same, but put a plank as a ramp from the lowest rung of the climbing frame ladder. Observe.
*Wednesday:* the same, but perhaps raise height, depending on how children respond.

*Figure 5.1* Example of a playgroup's weekly planning sheet.

*You might like to think about what the role of the adult is when children are busily engaged in exploring physical space? Do you think it is about ensuring that the children are safe or is there more involved?*

Many practitioners are so intent on ensuring that children are playing safely (which is, of course essential) that they ignore the possibilities inherent in the situation for intervening appropriately and scaffolding learning.

*Read through the case study below and then try and identify where you, the adult, might have intervened in order to extend learning. Try and say what you might have said or done.*

> Rehan, Jo, Beth and Akinola (who has very little English) are all four years old. They are out in the garden playing on the climbing frame. Rehan is 'in charge'. He is leading the other children and telling them what to do. They follow his suggestions happily until Beth, climbing up on to the plank which goes from one frame to another, loses her balance and nearly falls. She starts to cry and Jo rushes over to comfort her. Akinola, meanwhile, climbs down, goes inside and fetches a cushion from the book corner which he places underneath the plank. He urges Beth to have another go. She refuses and goes indoors. Jo, meanwhile, starts to hang upside down from the rungs and swings to and fro, shouting 'My head's down! My head's down!' Akinola climbs down and stands beneath Jo watching her in fascination. Then he climbs up again and attempts to hang upside down.

*How did you get on?*

There are no right or wrong answers because we are all individuals and will see things differently and interact differently. But you will have seen many points at which you might have intervened. For example, Akinola's obvious concern for Beth and his action in fetching the cushion offered the opportunity for the adult to reflect back to him the importance of his action by saying something like, 'That was such a thoughtful thing to do, Aki. You were making sure that if Beth fell she wouldn't hurt herself.' Did you also consider the many opportunities in this example for introducing some of the language of position and comparison? Notice here the links with mathematical development.

This brings us to the early learning goal related to developing a sense of space.

*Show awareness of space, of themselves and of others.*

You can see how the children in the above example are exploring space and beginning to understand their own capabilities and those of their peers. Offering opportunities for the exploration of space on a large scale almost inevitably offers children opportunities for play together. Children need to be aware of other children as they climb and jump, run and ride bikes. They need to take turns on the climbing frame and negotiate who is going to do what. And as they play with other children they use language in a meaningful and active context. Listen to your children as they talk in their play and you will find evidence of this. Vygotsky reminds us that:

> Learning awakens a variety of internal developmental processes that are able to operate only when the child is interacting with people in his environment and in co-operation with his peers.
>
> (Vygotsky 1978)

A final word in this section about risk-taking. The concern for children's safety often overrides everything. Many practitioners place restrictions on children which limit their opportunities to explore fully. This is not always confined to the outdoor area. Some practitioners limit the number of children who can play in the home corner or who can use the woodwork bench or who can be at the water tray. Such restrictions remove autonomy from the child and make the child dependent on the adult to define what is possible. You might like to remind yourself that one of the characteristics of play is that it allows children to take risks because children set their own agenda.

This is an area which often gives rise to fierce argument between practitioners. Obviously you need to ensure that the environment you provide is as safe as possible, but you also need to consider whether you have made it so safe that little learning can take place. It is important to allow children to take 'safe risks'. After all, if there are five children in the home corner rather than the four you have stipulated, what is the danger? The danger is that you, the adult, are less in control. The children will regulate themselves. When the home corner becomes too crowded play becomes difficult and the children have to resolve this situation for themselves – an excellent opportunity for problem-solving and negotiating. Similarly, when considering outdoor play, think carefully about whether you need to limit the numbers of children on the climbing frame or try to restrict what they do.

There are two early learning goals which relate to children becoming aware of health and their own bodies. These are:

*Recognise the importance of keeping healthy and those things which contribute to this.*

*Recognise the changes that happen to their bodies when they are active.*

These are interesting goals, which did not have equivalents in the earlier 'Desirable Outcomes'. In developing countries much more attention is paid to things like health and nutrition in terms of promoting children's learning and development. These early learning goals offer practitioners opportunities to think more carefully about a number of issues:

- the variety of family expectations and practices in terms of health and nutrition;
- the particular health needs of individual children, particularly those with special needs;
- involving children in understanding about the importance of basic hygiene procedures;
- promoting independence; and
- helping children learn to make choices and articulate these.

The final early learning goals for this learning area are:

*Use a range of small and large equipment.*

*Handle tools, objects, construction and malleable materials safely and with increasing control.*

The ability to use tools is essential to life. By tools we mean any of the huge number of objects we use as extensions of our hands in our everyday lives – things like a pen, toothbrush, pencil, broom, lawn-mower, computer and so on. Tools are an extension not only of our hands, but also of our minds. If you use a window pole to open a window the pole serves as an extension to your body and enables you to perform something you would not be able to do without using the tool. If you use a pen to write down some ideas the tool acts as an extension of your mind.

In the early years of life – the years described by Piaget as the Sensori-motor Stage – young children spend a great deal of time exploring the objects they encounter. They move on from asking, 'What is this thing? What does it do?', to asking, 'What can I do with this? What can I use it for?' By the time children start in the playgroup or nursery they have often had a great deal of experience of exploring the objects in their world and will continue to do so, refining their skills and enhancing their learning.

It follows from this that skilled early years practitioners will pay a great deal of attention to the tools and objects they offer children and to the activities in which these tools and objects are set.

Let us return to Rainbow Playgroup and see how they organise for children's exploration of tools and materials.

The staff set up a graphics area (or writing table) and offered the children the following tools, all in labelled containers or set out on stencils:

pencils
a range of felt pens
crayons
ballpoint pens
rubbers
Tippex
scissors (both left- and right-handed)
a hole punch
a stapler
glue sticks
sellotape
masking tape
rulers

In the technology (or workshops area) the following tools are on offer:

various kinds of glue
assorted boxes, cartons and containers all sorted according to size and shape
large sheet of wrapping paper, foil, tissue paper
scissors
stapler
sellotape
masking tape
paste spreaders
elastic bands

In the woodwork area:

a woodwork bench
a vice
a saw
hammers
nails and panel pins
a selection of pieces of wood
wood glue

A variety of malleable materials (dough, cornflour and water, clay, etc.)

offered with all or some of the following:

a garlic press
a cheese grater
wooden rollers
pastry cutters
straws
cookie tins
knives
spoons
forks
objects that can be used for leaving an imprint (like Sticklebricks)

In the construction area:

a set of large Community Playthings blocks set out on stencils
a set of small Community Playthings blocks similarly organised
a railway set
several construction toys like Lego, Duplo, Mobilo, etc.
vehicles
two wooden planks to act as ramps
some shiny strips of linoleum
some rough strips of cardboard

In their planning notes the staff plan that some of these activities will be set up outdoors each day, offering children the opportunity to develop their fine motor skills both indoors and out.

*Do you feel that resources like this would be equally appropriate in reception classes?*
You will realise just how much thought has gone into planning the resources described above. Some of them are costly (like a woodwork bench and the Community Playthings blocks) but most are not and can easily be gathered together and maintained. It is important that resources are set out in such a way that children can follow their own plans through and find the resources they need without having to call on an adult. Of course adults do need to be on hand in order to interact, to help, to demonstrate sometimes, to observe what the children are doing and to scaffold learning.

The difficult question of safety arises again. Some practitioners are reluctant to let children use woodwork tools or to use things like a garlic press. Often children are offered scissors which are so blunt that they will not cut. If children are to explore tools and to get involved in the processes they have determined for themselves it is essential that they are offered tools that work and that are cared for. Of course there are dangers, but children are generally sensible and respond well to being given some autonomy. Practitioners need to show children how to use the tools and explain to them that a saw, for example, is sharp and has to be used with care. They also need to involve the children in caring for the resources so that the next time they want to use them they are still in working order.

You may be interested in two examples of children exploring tools which were observed in a nursery in Reggio Emilia:

> A table had been set out for the children with rulers, sellotape, long strips of paper, glue, shiny objects, pieces of cardboard, pairs of scissors and pencils. The children were free to use the materials in any way they chose. Some children spent more than two hours at the table, rolling up strips of paper and gluing them on to other surfaces.
>
> At the clay table a group of children were working with an adult trying to make human figures out of clay. The children were aged between four and six. The adult offered them some simple stands made of two pieces of wood at right angles to each other. This formed a sort of support around which the clay figure could be constructed. When the adult was asked what had prompted her to come up with this brilliant device, she said that she had noticed that the children had difficulty in constructing three-dimensional figures out of clay because the legs were often too thin to support the body. As a result the figures made by the children were often two-dimensional and the children quickly lost interest in making these, since their intention had been to make three-dimensional figures.

## Summing it up

You will all already offer children many opportunities to explore the physical world. The important points to remember are that children need access to as many experiences as possible in order that their learning continues – in other words, in order that they are able to gain increasing control of both their fine and gross motor skills. You will want to consider how you can offer a safe and stimulating environment which allows children to take 'safe' risks.

- Children, from a very early age, explore the physical world through movement and through the exploration of the objects they encounter.
- Physical development has consequences for all aspects of development – cognitive, linguistic, social and emotional.
- Practitioners need to ensure that children are able to develop and refine their existing skills through a carefully planned programme and thoughtful resourcing.
- The role of the adult is more than a supervisory role. As in all areas of learning, adults need to observe, to scaffold learning, to interact, to

demonstrate, to explain, to listen, to offer help and to support in as many ways as possible.

- Although it is essential to ensure that children play and learn in a safe environment, thought needs to be given to allowing children to take risks in order to become autonomous.
- Practitioners will want to pay attention to the range of tools and materials they offer to children.
- Collaborative play is easily fostered through physical play, particularly outdoors.
- Practitioners will want to explain to children how to use tools safely.
- Practitioners will want to involve children in caring for the equipment in their nursery or playgroup.
- Tools and equipment that are not properly cared for insult the child and limit the children's abilities to fulfil the purposes they have set in their play.

## References

Abbott, L. and Rodger, R. (eds) (1994) *Quality Education in the Early Years*, Buckingham, Open University Press.

DfEE and QCA (2000) *Curriculum Guidance for the Foundation Stage*, London, DfEE.

Greco, P. (1962) 'Quantité et quotité', cited in C.K. Williams and C. Kamii, (1986) 'How Do Children Learn by Handling Objects', *Young Children*, November.

Gura, P. (1996) 'An Entitlement Curriculum for Early Childhood', in S. Robson and S. Smedley (eds), *Education in Early Childhood*, London, David Fulton.

Robson, S. and Smedley, S. (eds) (1996) *Education in Early Childhood*, London, David Fulton.

Vygotsky, L. (1978) *Mind in Society: The Development of Higher Psychological Processes*, Cambridge, MA, MIT Press.

# Chapter 6

# Exploring the world and expressing ideas

We have looked at how children seek to understand the world and the objects in it. They also seek to understand and explain wider aspects of the world. They ask questions about how things happen and why: they want to know how things used to be; they want to know what it is like in places they encounter in books, on television or through family links. And through their explorations they attempt to express their ideas and thoughts and feelings as they represent what they learn. In the Foundation Stage two areas of learning are involved: 'knowledge and understanding of the world' and 'creative development'.

In terms of coming to develop the skills, knowledge and understanding to help them make sense of the world children need activities based, as always, on first-hand experiences that will encourage them to observe, question, make guesses, try things out, solve problems, make predictions, identify patterns, think critically and discuss. This means that practitioners need to set up challenging activities inside and out, activities which are imaginative and enjoyable and open-ended. Adults need to consider how they can help the children express their ideas and to assess children's progress as they do in all other learning areas.

When considering children exploring the natural and made worlds there are a number of early learning goals, as follows:

*Investigate objects and materials by using all of their senses as appropriate.*

*Find out about and identify some features of living things, objects and events they observe.*

*Look closely at similarities, differences, patterns and change.*

*Ask questions about why things happen and how things work.*

What we are considering here is what can be called the 'scientific process'. Anyone who encounters something new, unfamiliar and interesting, struggles to understand it. Young children want to know all sorts of things like why hair grows and grows, how babies are made, why things with wheels roll, why things that are dropped always fall to the ground. In order for them to ask these questions they have to have gone through this scientific process. Let us take the example of the child wondering why things that are dropped always fall to the ground and examine the processes involved.

Basically, what happens is that the child observes something which raises a question in the child's mind. The child notices that an object, when dropped, always falls to the ground. So the child decides to see whether this applies to only some objects or to all objects. The child spends hours (maybe even days) dropping large and small objects. In doing this the child is testing out his or her hypothesis. At some point the child realises that all objects, when dropped, will fall to the ground. In other words the child has arrived at some sort of conclusion.

This process – observing, questioning, hypothesising, testing and conclud-ing – is what scientists do as they try to uncover some of the laws and patterns of the physical and natural worlds. Susan Isaacs ran a school in the 1920s which was structured around the principle that young children should be offered a rich and stimulating environment in which they would encounter problems to excite their imaginations and invite them to find solutions. The staff at the Malting House School were all trained to observe children closely and to let children follow their own interests. Susan Isaacs herself wrote a fascinating book (now sadly out of print) in which she records some of the observations and gives dramatic evidence of children learning and developing through their own explorations and the responses of the adults. One of her most fascinating examples concerns the death of one of the rabbits at the school. When the children came in one morning and found the rabbit lying in its hutch they discussed whether or not it was dead. Then one of the children said he knew how to find out. He said they needed to put the rabbit in water to see if it floated. His hypothesis was that dead things sink and living things float. The children put the rabbit in the water and noticed that it moved in the water. They concluded that the rabbit was still alive. Now Susan Isaacs, working with these children, helped them make the next step in learning and understanding. She brought the children a twig, which all the children agreed was not alive. The children put the twig in the water and it, too, was moved by the currents in the water. The children were able to realise that it was the current which had moved the rabbit and that the rabbit was, indeed, dead. What happened next arouses strong feelings in some readers. The children buried the rabbit, but a few days later started to hypothesise about whether the rabbit was still underground or if it had gone 'to heaven'. Susan Isaacs allowed the children to dig up the dead rabbit, which they examined with great interest and a huge amount of passionate discussion.

The children in your setting will be behaving like little scientists in many situations. To stimulate their curiosity and learning you might like to consider what situations and resources will best enhance this learning. Here are some examples to illustrate ideas:

> At the Rainbow Playgroup they have paid attention to the resources they can gather together to offer opportunities for children to behave scientifically. The resources include things like batteries, bulbs, magnets, mirrors, motors and gears, pumps and torches, screwdrivers, sieves and tubes. They have gathered together collections of things – things that roll, things that reflect, things that stretch, things that are transparent. They ensure there is a good range of natural objects, living things, found objects and to help children refine their skills of observation they supply midispectors and magnifying glasses. To help children explore sound they offer things to bang, to pluck, to vibrate, to scratch and to shake.

> Staff in one of the nursery classes at Amandla School noticed that children's play in the sand had become rather repetitive. They set out the sand in two small containers – one with wet sand and one with dry. On the table next to the trays they placed some miniature scoops, some tea-strainers, some shiny objects, some cut up straws and some small moulds.

> When the weather turned very cold the teacher in a reception class asked the children if they would like to do an experiment. She asked them to suggest what they could do to find out how ice is made. Following the children's suggestions and allowing them to select containers, a range of dishes and bowls was filled with water, fruit juice, and milk. Some containers were put outdoors; the others left indoors. The children then guessed what would happen and rushed in next morning to test out their hypotheses.

However flawed this activity is in scientific terms, it certainly allowed the children to raise questions, to get involved in designing an experiment, to hypothesise, observe and draw conclusions.

These early learning goals relate to finding and using resources and tools to carry out plans they have made:

*Build and construct with a wide range of objects, selecting appropriate resources, and adapting their work where necessary.*

*Select the tools and techniques they need to shape, assemble and join the materials they are using.*

ners will know how much children enjoy making or building
ild will happily spend a very long time making something totally
unrecognisable to the adult eye but deeply satisfying to the child. The process
involves planning what to make, choosing the materials and tools for the task,
making the environment or object, reviewing it and making changes where
necessary.

Here are two examples:

Donna is constructing in the brick area. She is trying to make a bridge.
She gathers together some cylindrical blocks and places them in a line
with spaces between them. She then gets a plank of wood to lay across
the top of them. The plank she has chosen is too short to cover all the
cylinders. She stops, looks carefully, tries the plank two or three more
times and then carefully removes two cylinders. This time the plank fits.

In the reception class all the children are being asked to make a card for
Mother's Day. They have all been given a piece of card and some pictures
they can cut out of magazines. They then copy the message from the
board.

*In which of these activities can you see evidence of the child planning what to make,
selecting the materials and evaluating what has been achieved?*

Children are only likely to get deeply involved in their construction and
making where they can make choices and find what they need. Here is how
Rainbow Playgroup set up a 'workshop area':

We ask parents to bring in materials for this on a regular basis. At first all
the empty cartons and boxes were just dumped into a large container, but
we discovered that the children were just taking the thing at the top and
not making proper choices. So we rearranged this and managed to get the
parents to put their offerings in the correct container. We have several
large plastic containers and they are labelled. All the toilet rolls and
long cylinders go in one: circles (lids and things like that) in another;
large boxes, small boxes, tubs and so on. Then we have made stencils and
put things on them: a stapler, sellotape, masking tape, pairs of scissors,
rulers and so on. We mix glue every morning and children know that
they can go and get the woodwork glue from the work bench if they
need it.

As well as all this we collect attractive things and store these in
labelled containers – things like sequins, beads, bits of fabric, cut up
wrapping paper, pictures, small objects the children bring in, feathers,
ribbon and so on. Then we also provide lots and lots of different sizes
and shapes of paper. We have rolls of foil, sheets of wrapping paper,
sheets of shiny paper and sheets of tissue paper. We explain to the

children that these are expensive and should be used with care. We were amazed at how responsive the children were. Sometimes we hear them saying things like, 'I'm going to use some of that 'spensive shiny stuff 'cos this is for my mummy!'

The technology area was the first area of our room we paid attention to and it remains very popular with the children. We often timetable an adult to be there, but even when no adult is actually based there we set it up in the mornings with something slightly different each day. The children spend a very long time in there, getting deeply involved in what they are making. We have noticed that it is an area where there is a lot of talk going on and are aware of the fact that, since it is not dependent on children being able to speak English, all the children in the room use it.

Within this learning area children are also expected to have opportunities to explore and use everyday technology as they work towards meeting this early learning goal:

*Find out about and identify the uses of everyday technology and use information and communication technology and programmable toys to support their learning.*

Not all settings have access to computers and many that do offer the computer as 'an activity', not necessarily thinking about how to use it as a tool for children to use to support their learning. There are now many programmes produced particularly for young children, but if you use these you need to examine them and consider just how they support learning.

Young children will enjoy just playing with the keyboard and watching what happens on the screen when they press keys. This physical exploration is an essential stage of learning, and children who do this are not 'messing about'. Adults can certainly interact with children as they explore the effects of their actions, explaining the purpose of keys and symbols. Older children may attempt to find particular significant letters on the keyboard – perhaps those to be found in their names. You will recognise that the symbols on the keyboard are upper-case letters; you may want to buy or make a template of lower-case letters to fit over the keys.

Young children will also enjoy the effects of using one of the many paint programmes available, particularly if you have access to a colour screen and colour printer.

There are a number of programmable toys and you may find that children are familiar with them and adept at using them. Here is an example from the reception class:

The class has two Roamers and the children play with them frequently. One of the nursery nurses decided to link this activity with a story she had been reading to the children. She brought in some props – a plastic castle, some plastic dinosaurs, a small doll, etc. and then made up a story about how the prince, in the Roamer, had to rescue the princess in the castle and to do so had to navigate round some obstacles. The children were deeply involved and totally engrossed and found programming the Roamer a meaningful thing that they could manage sometimes unaided.

Do remember that you routinely use tape-recorders, cameras, perhaps even digital cameras in your work with young children. These can be considered examples of everyday technology.

For young children, living primarily in the here and now, concepts about time are difficult and there is little to be achieved by introducing topics such as 'A Victorian Classroom'. But young children are interested in their own lives and the lives of people close to them and some interesting things can be done around these themes to meet this early learning goal and those associated with where children live:

*Find out about past and present events in their own lives and those of their families and other people they know.*

*Observe, find out about, and identify features in the place they live and the natural world.*

*Find out about their environment and talk about those features they like and dislike.*

Lettie, one of the practitioners in the playgroup, has brought in a photograph of herself as a baby. She has also collected some baby things for the children to explore. She is hoping that the children will start talking about the new baby at home or about when they were babies. She plans to ask parents to bring in photographs of their own children as babies and has invited Dario's mother to bring her new baby in to show the children. She also plans to set up a baby clinic in a corner of the room. The children arrive and all cluster round her picking up the bibs and bottles and baby clothes and are very intrigued by the photograph. 'Look,' shouts Sam in glee, 'no hair.'

'I didn't have hair when I was a baby,' responds Lettie, 'but then it grew and now I have got long hair, haven't I?'

'My baby got hair,' contributes Filiz, who very rarely says anything since she is in the early stages of acquiring English.

*What can you do to help children develop their ideas and knowledge about their own world?*

Many playgroups, nursery and reception classes build outings into their programme. These can range from outings to the local shops in order to buy the materials for cooking or to the local park or to travel on local transport. Visits such as these allow children to make the links between home and nursery and to build on their prior experience. Older children will enjoy visits to places of interest – perhaps to a building site or to a museum or to see a place of particular local interest. You would obviously link the visit to the children's interests and the ongoing work of the nursery group. In doing this you will think about what you can do, before the visit, to prepare the children to get the most out of it. You will also consider what to do within your setting after the visit in order to allow children to build on the experience. Here are some examples of what practitioners in different settings have done:

We took the children to the fire station and I took along a camera. When we got back the children all wanted to draw pictures and we agreed that we would make a big book about the visit. We used both photographs and children's drawings and the children, with my help, constructed the text which I wrote up in big print in front of them. This gave them a model of how writing works. I also made sure that I had got together some resources for them to use in their imaginative play – some plastic helmets, two small ladders and lots of lengths of hose-pipe.

We took the children to the local market where there is a stall that sells seeds. When we got back we set up a plant stall and the children all planted their seeds and labelled them (using invented writing or copying the letters on the seed packets). We talked about how plants need water, and the children were really reliable about looking after their plants. They put prices on them and got out the till and the plastic money. One child got some wrapping paper from the technology area to wrap up the plants she was selling. The next day a parent brought in armfuls of cut flowers which the children could also sell at the stall. It was a great success.

Next to the school there is a lot of building going on. I arranged with the site manager to take a group of children across. The children were fascinated with what was going on. When we got back we set up a section of the garden as a construction site. I got together some pairs of Wellington boots, some shovels and forks and some safety helmets. The children carried over planks of wood and large wooden blocks. Two children set up a 'site office' and asked me for some clipboards. The play went on for weeks and involved a great deal of talk and a lot of writing. It was brilliant!

In addition to planning outings and their follow-up, you will want to ensure that you have some books which will extend children's learning about their world. There are many excellent information books available for young children. If you do not already own these in your setting and if funds are limited, you can borrow them from the library. So, if you have set up a baby clinic, you might want to borrow books about babies, if you have set up a garage, you might want books about cars and vehicles. And do remember that things like DIY manuals, placed in your imaginative play areas, will spark off a great deal of talk and exploration.

At this point it is important to remind ourselves of a principle of early learning – and that is that young children need to be able to see the significance of what they are doing. In other words, they need to make the links between their lives and their experience and what is offered to them. History, for young children, is very brief – perhaps only as long as their own lives. Similarly young children will want to explore their immediate and slightly wider environment, and where you have children in your group who have been born in other countries or who have travelled abroad, setting up an aeroplane or turning your home corner into a non-traditional non-English home may be very effective. The key is to link what you offer to the children's experience so that they can build on this. This brings us back to the essential tenet of good early years practice – that it builds on individual children's needs, experience and interests and allows children, in situations that make human sense to them, to learn through play and with the sensitive support of adults.

Visits will also help children discover the purposes of some of the features they notice in their environment. Young children, starting in your setting, will already have discovered that shops are there to sell things, that banks are there for people to get money from, that bus stops are where people wait when they want to take a bus. You can build on this knowledge by reproducing some of these features within your setting. Some playgroups have noticed just how play is sustained when they have set up things like a post office, a garage, a bus station, a restaurant or a supermarket within the setting.

The final early learning goal for this learning area is:

*Begin to know about their own cultures and beliefs and those of other people.*

You will see the links between this and some of the goals for personal, social and emotional development. You will also, I hope, notice that once again there is no mention of language. Here are some incidents recorded in nursery classes, playgroups and reception classes across the country. Which do you think will enable children to learn to celebrate their own cultures and develop respect for those of others?

The class has an assembly for Mother's Day and all the children sing a song in assembly about 'Mummy does the cooking' and 'Mummy does the washing'.

The project in the reception class is 'bread' and each week a different type of bread is baked, often with the help of parents and family or community members.

There is a collection of musical instruments from around the world that children have constant – and noisy – access to.

Andy comes home from school and demands to be christened and is horrified to hear that she cannot be because her family is Jewish.

## Summing it up

- Knowledge and understanding of the world encompasses a very wide area of learning and development. Providing for this learning is a vital part of the role of all practitioners and one of the best ways of doing this is to remember that children learn best where they are able to see the point of what they are doing and where they are able to build on what they already know.
- As young children strive to understand their world they want to know about how and why things happen; about people and their relationships; about their own lives and families both now and in the 'touchable' past.
- Practitioners will want to help children find answers to the questions they raise by setting up meaningful contexts within the setting; using appropriate information books and taking children on visits and outings into the local community.
- Practitioners will show an interest in children's developing ideas and concepts and will encourage children to talk about these in context rather than in testing situations. They will also provide materials for the children to use to record their ideas should they wish to do so.
- Practitioners will want to ensure that they provide many opportunities and resources for children to behave like little scientists.
- They will also offer an environment which supports children making choices in terms of materials and resources.
- Access to technology should be part of everyday activities.
- Practitioners need to remain alert to ensuring equality of access and opportunity within all the activities on offer.
- Care should be taken to ensure that what is talked about, represented and offered allows all children to learn more about their own and others' cultures, beliefs and languages.

## Creative development

You will remember that Loris Malaguzzi talked of 'the hundred languages of children', by which he meant the many ways in which children can express their ideas and thoughts and findings (see p. 46). Young children need to be able to explore the world and express their findings in as many different ways as possible. This representation and re-representation of their ideas is an essential ingredient in learning.

In our society – and particularly in our schooling – we tend to place a far greater emphasis on the skills of reading, writing and numeracy than we do on the creative areas of music, dance and art, for example. Yet if you consider what enriches your life, you will probably include things like listening to music, looking at pictures, going to the cinema or theatre, or dancing. The music you enjoy and the films that please you may be different from those that please your best friend – but one of the things that makes us human is that we are moved by the ways in which other people are able to express their thoughts and ideas and feelings using whatever means they choose. You may also have come across the work of Howard Gardner who talks of *multiple intelligences*. He says that we all learn differently and that our schooling system should allow for this. Our schooling system focuses primarily on reading and writing and counting, but there are many children who learn best through physical exploration and others who learn best through dance or drama.

Young children who are fortunate enough to grow up in a society which values creative expression are exposed from an early age to things of beauty. The children, cited in an earlier chapter, visiting the cathedral in Modena, were able not only to look at beautiful things but to have a go for themselves at expressing their ideas through drawing, painting, mime, dance, imaginative play, music and three-dimensional work. Each attempt at re-describing or re-representing ideas refined children's concepts. It is important to remind ourselves at this point of the importance of what Malaguzzi describes as 'the journey' that children take as they attempt to represent their ideas and feelings. This, the process, is what determines the quality of the learning. The better the journey, the deeper the learning. This applies to children making marks on paper, constructing three-dimensional objects or structures, moving in response to music or any other situation in which children become deeply engaged in expressing their ideas, thoughts and feelings.

Let us now look in detail at the early learning goals for this learning area:

*Explore colour, texture, shape, form and space in two and three dimensions.*

*Respond in a variety of ways to what they see, hear, smell, touch and feel.*

In considering the opportunities you already provide for ∉ their world and the objects in it, you will become aware tha. learning goal refers not only to creativity, but also to exploration an. mathematics and physical development. Young children, being inhere. curious, explore everything they encounter. In doing so they inevitably pay attention to how things are similar and how things are different. A child presented with three balls, two of which are blue and one green, will perhaps pay attention to colour. The child offered three balls, one rubber, one wool and one plastic may pay attention to texture. This goal offers a good example of just how difficult it is to describe young children's learning in terms of subject areas or areas of learning.

It follows from this that children need to be in an environment in which there are interesting things to explore. In the Italian nursery schools described earlier staff collect 'beautiful' things for the children to touch, to examine and to explore. Together with these they offer a range of magnifying glasses and materials for painting, drawing, and three-dimensional work. You may want to think about how you can give children the experience of seeing paintings or sculpture or artefacts. One way to do this is to take children on outings to interesting places. Some nurseries take small groups of children to art galleries and museums. Many offer very appropriate programmes for young children. Another way is to get together a collection of posters, books or post-cards. A third way is to invite parents to bring in objects that they find interesting or beautiful and to share these with the children. In one nursery school a teacher collected various artefacts from her holiday and brought these in for the children to touch and look at. They were simple things like shells, a length of batik fabric, a small doll, a local musical instrument.

Do the children in your setting listen and respond to music? Young children hear music all around them and many children respond to music by singing, moving to the music, using parts of their body to emphasise the rhythms. Do try and ensure that your children are invited to listen to many different types of music. It is easy nowadays to get hold of tapes of music from all over the world and you might want to think about putting a tape-recorder with a selection of taped music in the home corner. Some prac-titioners still have a 'ring time' and in one setting this was often used as the time to introduce a tiny snatch of classical music to the children. Whilst the children were passing round their morning fruit, the teacher put on a brief excerpt of music and talked to the children about it. Even the youngest children were responsive.

Think of what you can provide to ensure that children can respond to what they hear and smell, see, touch and feel. Here is what they do at Amandla Early Years Unit:

> We sometimes use an object that someone has brought in or found and that they find interesting and then provide magnifiers or mirrors and

lots of art materials – different kinds of paper, pencils, pens, charcoals, paints, pastels and perhaps collage materials for depicting texture. And we talk about how things look, how they feel, how they make us feel. We make books about things. There is a wonderful one about lemons with children saying things like, 'It makes my mouth go tight when I taste it', or, 'The skin is lumpy and bumpy and pale and smells nice.'

*Use their imagination in art and design, music, dance, imaginative and role play.*

*Express and communicate their ideas, thought and feelings by using a widening range of materials, suitable tools, imaginative and role play, movement, designing and making and a variety of songs and musical instruments.*

*Recognise and explore how sounds can be changed, sing simple songs from memory, recognise repeated sounds and sound patterns and match movements to music.*

We want children not only to respond to the creations of others, but to have as many opportunities as possible to be creative themselves – that is to express their own thoughts and feelings in any way they choose. We are back to the 'hundred languages of children'.

You will want to ensure that, in your setting, children are able to express their personal feelings through art (painting, drawing, collage, using clay, making things), through music (singing, playing musical instruments and making up their own musical patterns), through movement (responding to sounds and music, using gesture and mime and dancing) and through story (responding to stories, creating their own stories and acting out stories in their imaginative play).

Let us take each of these areas in turn and suggest what materials and activities might promote children's learning.

## Art

John Matthews (1994) examines young children's drawing and painting and shows, in his book, how these expressive acts can play a central role in the development of cognition or understanding and in the development of feelings.

Matthews looked at his own children's development and paid close attention to exactly what it was the children were attempting to describe or express. He noticed that the children's involvement in their painting and drawing was deepened where the adult concerned was able really to tune into whatever it was the child was paying attention to. Matthews reminds us that not all paintings or drawings are representational. They may not aim to represent something, but may simply reflect the child's absorption in the effects of his or her own movement, or the effect of mixing colours or what happens when two shapes are placed close together. This is an important point and one that many adults find difficult to grasp. We are so used to considering paintings as being 'of something' that we focus almost entirely on the end-product.

Let us look at an example to see how the involvement of the adult can affect the involvement of the child:

> Four-year-old Martin was drawing in the playgroup. The adult came over and asked him what he had drawn. He ignored her, folded up his piece of paper and went outside to play.
>
> The next day an adult was seated in the painting area of the playgroup observing two children. Martin came over and asked what she was doing. She explained that she was watching what the children were doing because she was interested in them. Martin put on an apron and proceeded to paint a thick red line around the edges of the paper. He then chose yellow and made some yellow dabs in the centre of his 'frame'.
>
> 'I like those dabs you are doing, Martin,' commented the adult.
>
> 'Yeah,' said Martin, picking up the brush in the green paint, 'and now I'm doing green dabs – dab, dab, dab.'
>
> He stood back to observe his painting. Then he carefully selected the red brush again and started to paint a series of vertical lines. 'These are lines,' he announced.
>
> 'You have done a red frame and now you are doing red lines,' commented the adult.
>
> 'And then I am going to do some red dabs.'

You will have noticed how the adult, by commenting on what Martin was doing, was able to maintain his interest and let him make choices and decisions. In this way the language the adult used scaffolded Martin's learning and allowed him to be able to reflect on what he was doing. His interest in the activity was sustained through the adult attention. By contrast, where the adult questioned Martin about what his pictures was of, he lost interest and left the drawing area.

You will want to ensure that you offer children high-quality materials that are properly cared for and you will want to involve children in caring for these materials. Here is a list of what you might want to provide:

✓ surfaces to paint on (sometimes easels, sometimes on the floor or table: paint behaves differently on an easel from on a horizontal surface);

✓ a range of types of paper (paint, crayons and pens produce different effects on absorbent paper, shiny paper, cartridge paper, etc.);

✓   felt pens of different thickness; pencils; drawing pencils; water colour; poster paint; finger paint; acrylic paint; charcoal (each requires a different technique and produces a different effect);
✓   thick and thin paint brushes; paint rollers;
✓   clay and tools for using with clay;
✓   materials for making things.


## Music

You will want to encourage various things in providing opportunities for children to explore music. Firstly you will want to help children, through listening to music, to respond in a personal and creative way. So you will want to offer children opportunities to listen to a range of music and respond to their reaction to the music in a way which focuses on what the child is paying attention to. You may comment on the fact that the child is clapping in time to the music, or that the child has noticed that the music is fast or that the child feels that the music makes him or her feel sad.

You will want to offer children opportunities to make music for themselves. You will ensure that singing songs is an integral part of your curriculum and that you include in your songs those reflecting the languages and cultures of the children. You will want children also to have access to a range of things to pluck, bang, scrape, blow, shake and vibrate. There are many very attractive musical instruments available nowadays and many of these will be familiar to children from their own homes and communities. It is important that children have ongoing access to these instruments. It is only through their own explorations of the instruments that they will discover what the instruments do and what the effects of their own body movements will have on the instruments. You may want to offer children opportunities to make their own musical instruments and to have a go at 'writing' music just as they 'write' stories. In order to do this you would make sure that children can find examples of written music (song books provide an excellent example) and that they have manuscript paper on which to write.

Here are some examples of how some settings make music an integral part of their curriculum:

> We went on a course where we learned some musical games to play with the children. So at story-time we often incorporate these games in our session. One of them involves singing a song around the group about the children's names. We sing 'My name is Annie. What is your name?' and the child sings back 'My name is Nikiwe. What is your name?' and points to another child. Then we sometimes give the children instruments and ask them to follow the 'conductor' who uses her hands to

signal loud and soft – raising the hand means loud, lowering means soft. On one occasion we asked the children to find anything in the room that would make a sound (and we had removed the instruments). They were amazing. They brought spoons to bang together, elastic bands to vibrate, blocks to knock together, corrugated card to strike, paper to crinkle. And sometimes we tell them to watch the conductor and to join in when the conductor points to them. Then sometimes we start off with a rhythm, just using body-parts, and ask them to join in.

We now have a music corner and have in there our tape-recorder and a selection of tapes. We have a range of musical instruments (bought out of the proceeds of our last jumble sale). We have made a 'music collage'. This is a large piece of card on which we have stuck things that will make a sound. We have a piece of corrugated card with a lollipop stick hanging next to it on a piece of string; milk-bottle tops which jangle against each other; and a range of other things to bang, pluck, scrape and rattle.

We used the song 'Ten Green Bottles' as the starting point for a series of activities. The children all know the song and we often act it out. Then we made a Big Book of it and the children drew the pictures. Then we got ten green bottles and filled them with different amounts of water and set them out (making sure they were in a safe place) together with some beaters. The children were fascinated by how they could 'make tunes' by playing the bottles.

## Dance

The exploration of space, using their bodies, is an essential part of early learning for most children. Where children have music to listen and respond to and are encouraged to move – in any way they choose – to the sounds they hear, they use movement as a way of expressing their own ideas and feelings. Some practitioners believe that any movement or dance session needs to be highly structured. You will have to make your own decision about this. These contrasting examples might help you in this:

All the children have taken off their shoes and socks for a 'dance' session. The adult gets them all sitting quietly on the floor and tells them she is going to play them some music and she wants them to listen to the music and move 'quietly'. She also reminds them that when she claps her hands they must all stop and sit down. She takes the children through a series of movements – moving slowly and quickly, moving high up and low down, tiptoeing and stamping. She often models the movements for the children.

The practitioner invites any children who want to come and dance to join her in the small room. The children take off their socks and shoes. Music is already playing when they come in and the children join in enthusiastically, each moving in their own way to the movement. The adult moves amongst the children, commenting on what they do. 'Marko, what a huge leap you made' and 'I love the way you are twisting your arms to the music'. When the short excerpt comes to an end she invites the children to suggest what sort of music they want next. One suggests 'loud'; another shouts out 'Bob Marley' and a third says 'songs'. A decision is reached and the children, again, move to the music. Finally, the worker tells the children she has brought in some new music – something she really likes and that reminds her of when she was a little girl and used to go to the seaside with her grandparents. She plays the tape and the children listen, some clapping, some joining in the song.

## Stories and imaginative play

You may have come across the work of Vivien Paley who uses storytelling as the main means of learning in her classroom. She encourages the children to make up their own stories in order to make sense of their lives and her books (which are fascinating and easy to read) show just how powerful storytelling is in terms of learning and reflection. Paley, through a long personal struggle, discovered that offering children opportunities to construct and act out stories allowed them to confront many issues in their lives and sort out their responses to these. She also discovered that children, in acting out through play, offered her a window into their development.

You will already offer children many opportunities to make up stories as they play in the home corner or other areas in your room. Try and ensure that the props you offer help to take children's storying and their learning forward. Younger children, more concerned with re-enacting domestic roles, will need access to 'real' things to help their play, but older children can use lengths of fabric, strips of hose-pipe, empty containers – anything, in fact – to become whatever they desire.

Please remember that it is important for you, as practitioners, to take careful note of what children are doing so that activities can be provided to help them refine their skills and increase their range of experiences. Each representation and re-representation contributes to learning and the more the opportunities for expressing feelings and thoughts, and the more sensitive intervention of the adult, the more chance there is that children will develop the abilities to use their imagination, to listen and to observe.

## Summing it up

- The things that enrich our lives are often things which arise out of our own creative efforts or of those of other people, yet in our schools the expressive aspects of learning have a low status. In our settings for young children we can remedy this by ensuring that creative development is as important to us as cognitive development.
- Young children need as many opportunities as they can get to try and describe and represent their ideas and feelings.
- When children are engaged in representing and re-representing their thoughts and feelings they are involved in solving problems, in selecting appropriate tools and materials, in cognitive development.
- The journey the child takes in representing thoughts and feelings is as important or even, some would argue, more important than the final destination. In other words, although the product matters it may well be the process that is important to the child.
- Children need to experience and explore painting and drawing, music, movement and dance, gesture and mime, storytelling and imaginative play. These should be regarded as some of the 'hundred languages' of children.
- The role of the adult is, as ever, complex. It involves setting up the environment and resources; modelling; using language to scaffold learning; offering help and advice where needed; tuning in to what it is the child is paying attention to; intervening sensitively.

## References

DfEE and QCA (2000) *Curriculum Guidance for the Foundation Stage*, London, DfEE.
Gardner, H. (1993) *Frames of Mind: The Theory of Multiple Intelligences*, New York, Basic Books.
Gura, P. (ed.) (1992) *Exploring Learning: Young Children and Block Play*, London, PCP.
Isaacs, S. (1930) *Intellectual Growth in Children*, London, Routledge and Kegan Paul.
Matthews, J. (1994) *Helping Children to Draw and Paint in Early Childhood*, London, Hodder and Stoughton.
Paley, V.G. 'On Listening to What Children Say', *Harvard Educational Review*, 56(2).

# Chapter 7

# Ensuring equality of access and opportunity

Meeting the diverse needs of children is an underpinning principle of the Foundation Stage and of all good early-years practice. Ensuring that all children – whatever their background, their experience, their gender, their culture, their religion, their ability – are offered equality of access and opportunity to the curriculum and to your time is something most practitioners strive to achieve. Starting with a knowledge of the children in the group and keeping in mind each individual when planning is the best way to do this.

Practitioners will want to:

- plan opportunities that build on and extend children's knowledge, experience, interests and skills;
- ensure that the opportunities help build children's self-esteem and confidence;
- use a wide range of teaching strategies that are directly related to children's observed and assessed needs and to their interests;
- set up an environment free of harassment and where racial, religious, disability and gender stereotypes are challenged;
- hear, respect and value the contributions of all;
- reflect the diversity within the group, the community and the wider society in all the resources and activities;
- monitor the progress of individual children and seek appropriate help and support where needed.

In provision, in planning and in review we need to think very carefully about children who have special educational needs or disabilities; about children with English as an additional language; about children from different ethnic groups and about girls and boys. We need to ask some difficult questions, including whether provision that is developmentally appropriate (which is what we are advocating) automatically addresses the needs of all children or whether some of what are regarded as 'the truths' about early childhood include some myths which may be damaging. If you are particularly interested in this you might want to read Glenda MacNaughton's book *Rethinking Gender in Early Childhood Education* (2000).

## Politically correct or educationally essential?

Have a quick look around your room and ask yourself what it feels like to be a girl, a black child, a child from a working-class family, a child who is a refugee, a child whose home language is not English. Can you, as this child, find things that are familiar? Do you see images of children like you?

*Why bother to consider issues of equality and access? You might want to jot down why you think it is important.*

There are many reasons. Some of these are personal or professional in nature (as where, for example, you believe that you have a professional duty to cater for all the children you care for) or even moral and human in intention (as where, for example, you believe that as a human being it is incumbent upon you to make sure that all children are treated equally). Many are actually grounded in legal requirements. In other words, considering the opportunities for all children is not something you can just choose to do in order to be 'right on' or politically correct. You have a legal obligation to do so under several acts of law.

The Children Act (1989) states that 'Children have a right to an environment which facilitates their development' and then goes on to address children's rights in terms of their sense of identity, which includes the right to individuality, respect, dignity and freedom from discrimination. If, in answering the questions that started this section, you felt that some children in your group might not feel that their particular sense of identity was overtly respected, you need to question whether you are, indeed, offering genuine equality of access and opportunity.

The Rumbold Report (DES 1990) insists that each institution should have:

(a) a policy outlining aims and objectives based on a clearly articulated philosophy shared by educators and parents. This should incorporate:
(b) a policy on equal opportunities for children and adults, encompassing gender, race, class and disability, which promotes an understanding of cultural and physical diversity and challenges stereotypes and which is responsive to local needs . . .

You can see from all of this that you need to have a policy on anti-discrimination or equity which you, as a group of practitioners, have agreed on and which you have shared with both children and parents. This policy needs to look at a number of issues, as follows:

• Your own *attitudes and beliefs and prejudices*. This is the essential starting point. You cannot devise and implement a policy on equal opportunities until you have examined and sometimes challenged your own views and ideas.

- A *clear understanding of the children in your care* – their home backgrounds, previous experiences, religious and cultural values, languages spoken, and other aspects of experience.
- A survey of *the resources you provide* in order to examine them for stereo-typical images and for monocultural or monolingual bias. In other words, do the books, jigsaws and pictures show positive images of girls, of black children, of children with disabilities, of boys, of working-class children? Can children find examples of their home languages in the books or tapes or wall displays in your room? Are images of Africa, for example, true to life, or do they depict Africa as a place where wild animals roam and people live in mud huts?
- A survey of *the activities you offer* in order to assess whether they invite all children to partake or in some way suggest that certain activities are only open to certain children. Obvious examples are areas like the home corner (do boys play there?) and the block play area (do girls play there?).
- An exploration of how you *handle incidents* like name-calling, bullying and teasing? Have you all agreed on a policy and do you all implement it equally?
- A consideration of *attitudes within your setting*. Ask yourself these questions: Do children feel valued? Do their parents feel valued? Are children beginning to be tolerant of the feelings of others? Do you foster co-operation rather than competition?
- A consideration of *how parents are involved* in the work of your setting.

Reading through this list you might believe that providing a curriculum based on meeting the observed needs of all the children in your group – a developmentally appropriate curriculum – will ensure that you offer equality of access and opportunity. But do remember that you need to take account of your own educational training, your understanding of each child, the strategies and resources you use, the views of parents, the views of children and the views of colleagues and peers. Here are some case studies to make this clear:

Julian is a male practitioner working with young children. He believes that his own experiences of growing up male in this society give him a particular viewpoint which he can use to help the boys he encounters. He spends a lot of time working with parents to help children deal with anger and aggression.

Henrietta is a black nursery nurse who works alongside a white teacher. She believes that her own experiences of discrimination gives her insights the teacher doesn't have and is keen that they work in partnership for the benefit of the children.

Iclal is a Turkish speaker who came to England with no English. Her first days in school have left a vivid impression on her and she draws on this to help the children in her class who have English as an additional language. She is very clear that dealing with discrimination means going beyond multiracial education.

Where you are aware of each child as an individual with a unique and important history and where you seek to build on this in the activities and resources you offer, you will be providing the broad and balanced curriculum recommended in The Rumbold Report. You do, however, need to know something about how social class, gender and race can provide the basis for discrimination if you are to have an effective and meaningful equal opportunities policy.

## Social class

It is a truism to say that those working with young children need to know the children well. What is sometimes ignored, however, is how this knowledge about children is acquired. Sometimes practitioners make judgements about children on spurious grounds. They judge that a child will not be successful in school, for example, if the child comes from the local council estate or if the child comes from a single-parent family or if the child's parents are unemployed. Attitudes like this reflect a deficit and stereotypical view of working-class families and often result in a self-fulfilling prophecy. Where a practitioner assumes that a child will fail, for example, that practitioner may fail to engage properly with the child's home experience, and in this way ensures that the child does fail. There are many studies you can read to illustrate this: Walkerdine et al. (1989), MacGilchrist (1992), Anning (1991).

One of the most obvious areas in which social class emerges as a factor is in terms of language. Some years ago it was believed that children coming from so-called working-class homes encountered an inferior form of language within their homes. Basil Bernstein, a sociologist, said that middle-class families used what he called an 'elaborated code' of language, whilst working-class families used a 'restricted code' of language. What he meant by this was that speakers using the restricted code were more dependent on the immediate context in which the language took place. Working-class children, he argued, always refer to things in the here and now, things that can be seen and touched and heard. Children exposed to the elaborated code, on the other hand, were able to move away from this and were not dependent on a shared context in order to communicate. Now since the language used in schools and in education is often about things that are not to do with the here and now and are not dependent on the current context, working-class children are at a disadvantage. This type of view – that of citing the blame for failure at school with the child and the child's family – is a deficit view and one that has been severely challenged since Bernstein's work. You have come across the work of Tizard and Hughes and of Gordon Wells and will know that they found that all homes provide language which enables children to talk, to think, to solve problems and to communicate.

Despite all this, deficit views of working-class families still prevail and it is still a fact that working-class children do less well within the educational system than those from more privileged homes.

## Gender

The process of learning about gender begins very early. Weis and Worobey (1991) believe that children, before the age of three, have already developed what they call 'scripts for their gender'. When you watch the children in your setting at play you may observe clear gender preferences in terms of what the boys and girls play with, who they play with and how they play. But because these gender preferences have already started developing does not mean that practitioners should be content to let them continue. Ways need to be found to allow those children who wish to explore alternative ways of playing and acting to do so. Certainly practitioners need to be aware of their own attitudes to gender and to watch carefully the models they offer and the language they use.

You may like to think about the contradiction implied when we say that children are active learners and when we say that children are socialised, at a very early age, into gender-specific roles. The latter is one of the myths we spoke of earlier in this chapter. It is important to always think of the individual child with regard to the social context within which that child learns and develops. Walkerdine *et al.* (1989) and Davies (1989) both see individuals as being both complex and multiple, and say that every individual constantly creates and recreates themselves through the different experiences, situations, interactions and discourses they encounter. This is a hopeful view and one that suggests that we should not describe girls as always being 'passive', for example. Girls may be passive in certain situations or with certain people, but if we allow ourselves to see them as 'complex and multiple', we will see that, in their play, they are often engaged in sorting out a power struggle with boys. They are acting out the power relationships they have observed and often challenging them. Just watch the girls in your home corner to see how powerful they can be.

The argument goes that simply providing things to attract girls to the construction area or boys to the home corner is not enough. What researchers suggest is that those working with young children need to pay close attention to the struggle children go through in their play and talk as they construct their own identities and learn who they are and where they are positioned. Through adult role-modelling, the use of drama and story and through positive intervention, both boys and girls can gently be challenged and powerfully supported as they come to an understanding of who they want to be.

## 'Race'

Historically, in Western Europe in particular, there has been a view that one race of people is genetically superior to another. This culminated, as you will know, in the extermination of six million Jews under Hitler's Nazi regime. Genocide and 'ethnic cleansing' continue to be tragic events as we begin the new millennium. In Britain the many groups of people who have come in from other countries have encountered active discrimination and prejudice: they have been encouraged to lose their cultures and languages in order to be assimilated into the host culture; they have been feted and treated as 'exotic' in some attempts at multiculturalism. Siraj-Blatchford (1994) argues that the only acceptable approach for those working with young children and their families is one which is genuinely anti-racist and one which is prepared to examine racial inequality on an institutional and on a personal level.

The colour of a person's skin is significant. It is not something that can be ignored or glossed over. Not all children are the same and it is deeply insulting to treat all children as though they were. Very young children are aware of difference and it is important that they have the opportunity to express their observations about difference and to come to an understanding that difference is something to celebrate and not something to jeer at or ignore. Young children, in coming to define their own identity, are inevitably influenced by other people's perceptions of them. If you are white and part of the white majority, your whiteness is not something you are acutely aware of. But if you are black and part of a black minority, your very blackness is part of what defines you.

Offering a curriculum which is multicultural is a start, but it does not go far enough if you are genuinely concerned to ensure equality of access and opportunity. What is required is ensuring that the community you create within your setting is one in which children can pursue their discovery of concepts of fairness and justice. Paley (1995) showed that young children are passionate enquirers and that their fears relate primarily to things like being left out, feeling inadequate and being unfairly treated. Paley suggests that through story (and by story she means the acting out of real or imaginary situations through play and talk) children can address these very deep concerns and come to very real understandings.

We will look now at Rainbow Playgroup's Equity Policy which was revised in March 2000.

This is the revised version of their original policy. They are keeping to their original agreement of revising and updating their work around anti-discrimination. As you read it please remember that, for the staff, the process of agreeing the policy was more important than the policy itself. Also remember that a policy as a piece of paper is worthless. It is the implementation and continual review of the policy which gives it life and meaning.

## Rainbow Playgroup

### Equity Policy

This is our first revision of the policy and has involved discussion at staff in-service training, with parents and with community leaders. The process of revision took three months.

### Aims

1   We aim to ensure that our environment is visually and emotionally welcoming to both children and their parents/carers.
2   We base our curriculum on The Curriculum Guidance for the Foundation Stage and aim to provide learning opportunities which: allow children to build on their previous experience; extend their knowledge and skills; foster their own interests; help build self-esteem and their own confidence in themselves as learners.
3   We aim to use a wide range of teaching strategies, based on what we know about each child through observation.
4   We aim to promote talking and language, including all the languages spoken by our children, in all the activities we offer.
5   We aim to offer a safe environment free of harassment in which the contributions of all children are valued explicitly.
6   We aim to challenge any racial, religious, disability and gender stereotypes and ensure that our resources are free of these.
7   We aim to use materials that positively reflect diversity and are free from discrimination and stereotyping.
8   We aim to promote respect for others through our own attitudes to the children, their parents and one another.
9   We aim to promote play as the primary mode of learning since where children can follow their own interests they are more likely to become deeply immersed in what they are doing.
10  We aim to promote cooperation and collaboration rather then competition.
11  We aim to ensure that we are alert to any signs of discrimination and as a staff, do not ignore such incidents or tacitly support them in any way.

### Operating the Policy

1   We will organise the playgroup so that our commitment to equality of access and opportunity is evident to all.
2   We will plan for and monitor the activities to ensure that no child is denied access to any activity on offer.
3   The resources we use and the activities we plan will reflect aspects of the community we serve. All activities will include resources and artefacts which will be familiar to the children and allow them to build on their prior experience.
4   We will continue to invite parents, carers and community members in to share their own skills, expertise and experience with us.
5   We will consider the very particular needs of children with special educational needs in our planning ensuring that we consider things like access, resources and support.
6   We will explain the policy to new parents, using translators and interpreters when necessary.
7   We will plan our meetings with parents at a time to suit their needs.
8   Our settling-in procedures will include inviting parents to bring a friend or older sibling to help with communication in English.
9   We will not allow any racist or sexist incident to pass unchallenged.

*NOTE: This policy will be reviewed each year. Any parent/carer wishing to contribute their views or ideas is invited to use the 'comments' box in the entrance hall. You may remain anonymous if you choose!*

## Children with special educational needs

*Do you have children with special educational needs in your setting? How do you know that these children have special educational needs? Do you know what these particular needs are? Do you know what your responsibility is in dealing with these children?*

In your setting you will have children whose development varies enormously. You may have a very tall four-year-old whose language development does not seem equivalent to that of other four-year-olds. You may have a tiny four-year-old who is extremely articulate, but who has difficulty with fine motor control. Children, as we know, vary enormously in their rate of development and in our zeal to describe children we sometimes label children as having 'special needs' or as being 'slow', 'naughty' or 'average'. Labels such as these suggest that we know something impossible – namely, that there is such a thing as 'average' or 'normal'. More importantly, these labels are usually negative and not very informative or precise and, what is more, they often become attached to the child. A child who is labelled at an early age as being a failure in some way carries the additional disadvantage of having to overcome this label.

At the other extreme, however, is the fact that the early detection of particular difficulties allows for early intervention. This means that you, working with young children, are in a position to be alert to signs of problems that young children may be having (perhaps only temporarily) and know how to respond to these.

This is a tremendous responsibility, but the law now provides a framework to help all those involved in some way with the education of children under the age of five to know what to do. The 1993 Education Act introduced a Code of Practice on the Identification and Assessment of Special Educational Need which lays out five stages leading up to the formal assessment and statement of those children identified as having special educational needs. The ways in which the process is carried out are left to the school or setting, but each must have a statement which is published and available to parents and managers or governors and each is required to have a nominated member of staff with special responsibility for special needs. This person, sometimes called the Special Educational Needs Coordinator, or SENCO, must keep a register of all children with special needs and a record of what has been done to meet these needs.

To help you, here is an outline of the five steps set out in the Code of Practice.

### Stage 1

This is the initial stage of gathering information and making some assessment of what the particular difficulty is. This is often initiated as the result of a parent, carer or worker expressing some concern about the child's development and is likely to be the stage most of you would be concerned with. It is important at this stage to liaise very closely with parents and to record in detail what the concern is, what steps have been taken and what the results are. It is recommended that practitioners, often together with parents, set targets for the child's progress and that these targets are also recorded. Other professionals may be involved at this stage – people like health visitors, speech therapists and so on. It is also recommended that reviews should be carried out, usually within a six-month period, and that if, after two such reviews, progress is not regarded as satisfactory (i.e. targets have not been met) Stage 2 is reached.

### Stage 2

This is the point at which you feel you need additional specialist advice from people like doctors, specialist teachers for children with hearing or visual impairments and so on. In this stage you are asked to draw up an Individual Educational Plan (IEP) for the child and this should include:

- the nature of the child's difficulties;
- any special provision given and by whom; any particular programmes followed;
- what help the parents give;
- targets to be achieved by particular dates;
- any medical arrangements or pastoral care;
- the arrangements for monitoring and assessment;
- the arrangements for review of progress.

Again, parents need to be kept fully informed and involved and their views should always be taken into account.

## Stage 3

During this stage the school or setting can call on additional professional help from people such as educational psychologists, and the responsibility for the child is now shared with any outside agencies called in. A new IEP is drawn up and, again, partnership with parents is essential. If, on review, progress is not satisfactory the child may be referred to the local education authority for a statutory assessment. The setting or school must provide written evidence of all that has been done during Stages 1 to 3.

## Stage 4

The local education authority is required to carry out a statutory assessment of the child within twenty-six weeks of a request to do so by a parent, a worker, a school or an outside agency. This is the point where the school or setting feels unable to promote the child's development within the school or setting.

## Stage 5

This is where a formal statement of the child's special educational needs is drawn up by the local education authority once it has established that the child's difficulties are:

- significant and/or complex;
- have not been met by the measures taken by the school or setting or support services;
- may call for resources which are not available within mainstream education.

You will see that this carefully structured framework does offer some support for practitioners attempting both to identify and cater for the needs of children.

## Summing it up

- Avoid labelling children.
- Be aware of the Code of Practice.
- Publish your policy on how your setting identifies children with special educational needs and sets about attempting to meet these.
- Identify a member of staff who will take particular responsibility for this area.
- Liaise closely with parents and deal sensitively with them.

## Working towards equity and equality

In this chapter we have started to examine the responsibility that all those working with young children have – morally, professionally and legally – to address issues of equality and equity for all children. This is an area that many practitioners find difficult to deal with because it sometimes forces them to face issues concerning their own view, beliefs and values. We all like to believe that we are without prejudice, yet confronting our innermost feelings sometimes reveals surprising and damaging things.

Within your setting you need to remember that you are empowered to create your own community. This community is bound to be influenced by the pressures and demands of the wider society, but it is possible to create a community which is socially just. You are in a position to influence the development of young children as social beings, initially within the social community of the setting or classroom, but equipping them to later look for justice in the wider community.

In all probability you will already have started doing some things towards achieving this goal. You may have looked at your resources in order to ensure that the images they offer are not stereotypes but show males and females and people from different cultures doing everyday, ordinary things. Images like this will allow the children both to build on their previous experience and to develop a sense of identity which they can be proud of. You will probably have thought about how you can support children whose first language is not English both in continuing to use that language, but also to acquire English. You may have thought of providing books in languages other than English; of using story-props to allow children into the meaning of the stories you tell and read; of displaying the alphabets and scripts used by the children and their families. You may have paid some attention to things like gender equality by considering what resources you offer in the home corner to encourage boys to play there; how you encourage girls to take active roles in outdoor play and block and construction play. You may have started to work closely with parents in order that you are able to understand their views and explain yours.

These aspects of ensuring equity and equality are important, but, in a sense, they are the ones that are relatively easy to do. In order that your policy has some 'teeth', however, there are some difficult things you have to do – and since these often involve changing attitudes, they take a long time. At William Patten Infants School in Hackney in the early 1980s the staff set about developing an anti-racist policy. After much debate and heart-searching, it was decided that the starting point had to be with the views of the staff. The staff split into two groups and each group met separately under the leadership of one of the teachers. The reason for the split was that those members of staff who were not teachers felt intimidated by the teachers and requested meeting on their own. Each group met regularly over a long period of time and the purpose was for each person, in turn, to relate their life story. There was only one rule – and that was that everyone had to listen and no one was allowed to interrupt. The point of doing this was for people who had previously been somewhat suspicious of those coming from a different cultural background to discover the things they had in common and to begin to develop an understanding of oppression.

So addressing issues of equality involves an examination of your own attitudes and also a willingness to consider factors of power and control that operate at a level beyond that of the individual. Weiner (1985) talks of the ongoing battle for power that exists between different groups – between men and women, between black and white people, between poor and rich. Inevitably, when considering such factors, one has to adopt a stance which is essentially political, and many people find this difficult.

But practitioners have an obligation to treat children as human beings and to deal with them seriously. In essence, anyone involved with young children, who are trying to understand the world and all its complexities, owes them the following:

- The presence of adults who are prepared to look objectively at their own practice to see how it affects different groups of children.
- A curriculum that values a range of cultures, languages and lifestyles.
- The provision of learning activities which allow children to explore ideas and concepts which will allow them to come to understand racism and other forms of oppression (Kidner 1988).

## References

Anning, A. (1991) *The First Years at School*, Buckingham, Open University Press.
Bernstein, B. (1974) *Class, Codes and Control*, London, Routledge and Kegan Paul.
David, T. (1990) *Under Five – Under Educated*, Buckingham, Open University Press.
Davies, B. (1989) *Frogs and Snails and Feminist Tales*, London, Allen and Unwin.

DfEE (1996) *Code of Practice on the Identification and Assessment of Special Educational Needs*.

DfEE and QCA (2000) *Curriculum Guidance for the Foundation Stage*, London, DfEE.

Kidner, J. (1988) 'Under Fives', in A. Cohen and I. Cohen (eds), *Early Education: The Pre-school Years*, London, PCP.

Long, P. (1996) 'Special Educational Needs', in S. Robson and S. Smedley (eds), *Education in Early Childhood*, London, David Fulton.

MacGilchrist, B. (1992) *Managing Access and Entitlement in Primary Education*, Stoke on Trent, Trentham Books.

MacNaughton, G. (2000) *Rethinking Gender in Early Childhood Education*, London, PCP.

Paley, V.G. (1995) *Kwanzaa and Me. A Teacher's Story*, Cambridge, MA, Harvard University Press.

Siraj-Blatchford, I. (1994) *The Early Years: Laying the Foundations for Racial Equality*, Stoke on Trent, Trentham Books.

Smedley, S. (1996) 'Working for Equality and Equity', in S. Robson and S. Smedley (eds), *Education in Early Childhood*, London, David Fulton.

Tizard, B. and Hughes, M. (1984) *Young Children Learning*, London, Fontana.

Walkerdine, V. and Girls from the Mathematics Unit (1989) *Counting Girls Out*, London, Virago.

Weiner, G. (1985) *Just a Bunch of Girls*, Buckingham, Open University Press.

Weis, D. and Worobey, J. (1991) 'Sex Roles and Family Scripts', *Early Childhood in Early Child Development and Care*, 77.

Wells, G. (1986) *The Meaning Makers*, London, Hodder and Stoughton.

# Chapter 8

# Documenting what children do

One of the most important things all teachers and practitioners do is observe children closely in order both to assess how well the children are learning and progressing and also to know how well their planning is meeting the children's needs. The *Curriculum Guidance for the Foundation Stage* has, as one of its principles, that practitioners *must be able to observe and respond appropriately to children*. This is broken down into three points:

- that practitioners make systematic observations and assessment of each child's achievements, interests and learning styles;
- that they use these observations and assessments to identify learning priorities and plan relevant and motivating learning experiences for each child;
- that they match their observations to the expectations of the early learning goals.

In the next section we will look in detail at how practitioners can do this.

## Observation

*Do you observe children regularly in your setting? How do you do this?*

In the best practice practitioners watch children carefully and listen to what they say. They often carry a pad and pen and jot down what they see and hear. At the end of the session or the day the trained practitioner then reads through each observation note and tries to interpret what has been seen and heard in terms of what the children demonstrate about what they know and can do. So as you observe, some questions may be raised in your mind. The answers to these questions not only help you to understand more about the children, but also give you an insight into how well you, the adult, are managing to support and extend children's learning.

Drummond (1998) says that observing children's learning is one of the most vital responsibilities of those who care for and educate children. When we observe children's amazing capacity for learning and development, it shows how much we must do in order to support, enrich and extend that learning. She goes on to say:

> Observing learning, getting close to children's minds and children's feelings, is part of our daily work in striving for quality. What we see, when we look closely, helps us to shape the present, the daily experiences of young children in all forms of early years provision. The act of observation is central to the continuous process of evaluation, as we look at what we provide and ask: is it good enough? Our careful observations of children's learning can help us make this provision better. We can use what we see to identify the strengths and weaknesses, gaps and inconsistencies, in what we provide. We can identify significant moments in a child's learning, and we can build on what we see.
>
> (Drummond 1998, p. 105)

Let us now examine how to ensure that observation is *systematic*. By this we mean that there is some system in place to ensure that all children are assessed and that observations follow some sort of plan. All those working with young children need to be involved in the observation and assessment process. If you operate a keyworker system, you will be primarily responsible for observing your key children. But in reality, in most settings, children move around so frequently that a practitioner may observe something very significant about a child who is not one of his or her key children. How you organise to observe children will be up to you as a staff group. There is no right way, but there are ways which are more efficient than others. Here are some examples:

> In our playgroup each practitioner chooses to look at four children over the week. She tries to observe those children in different activities and jots down notes as she does so. Then, on Friday, when the children have gone home we all sit down and summarise what we have seen about each of the children. If another practitioner has observed one of the target children doing something interesting she will add her comments.

> We vary what we do. At the moment we are observing the children in different areas. So my area this week is the home corner and I jot down notes about significant things that happen. Then we get together and share our observations.

> We've tried everything! At one point we seemed to spend our whole time writing and decided that that was not the best use of our time. At the moment we have organised the room so that in each area there are clipboards with pens attached, so that if something significant happens we

can record it. But we each take responsibility for observing three children per week.

Observation is time-consuming and demanding. Some practitioners found it difficult at first because they were worried about their hand-writing or their spelling. But we managed to persuade them that obser-vation notes were working notes and would not be seen by parents. We also decided that we had to be selective about what we noted and that we didn't have to write long sentences in perfect English. Most of our comments are brief – sometimes just a couple of words. Something like 'counted to two' or 'played with Emma'. But where we have concerns about a child we tend to try and do a more in-depth observation. And we also try and do an in-depth observation soon after the child has settled and then, for each child, perhaps one per term.

Can you see how there is a system for observing children in all these set-tings? All these practitioners are finding ways that suit them of observing and recording their findings. As you can see there is a great deal of trial and error involved as practitioners try and find what meets their needs.

Through your observations you will come across incidents that can be described as 'significant moments'. These are where a child does something for the first time. If you think about your own children's development or the development of children you know well, the things that stand out in your memory may be the so-called 'milestones' – the first word, the first step and so on. In terms of monitoring the development of the children in your care, you are looking for evidence of the child having moved on, having taken the next step in learning and development. Here are some examples of significant moments for different children:

- Paolo was very shy and withdrawn. I felt it was significant when I saw him approach another child, tug his arm and point to the car he was holding.
- Mariam was very unsettled at first, speaking no English. I felt it was significant when she stopped crying and joined in the play.
- Boris never ever chose to look at books. It was significant when he came in one morning and headed straight for the book corner.
- For Emilia, a significant moment was when she recognised her name in a Big Book we had made.
- For Joshua it was the first book he read from cover to cover.
- For Sacha, nearly six, it was the first time she read a book 'in her head'.
- It was significant when Josepha wrote the letter J in her made-up writing.
- For Hiram it was when he first wrote his name.
- For Jackson it was the first time he wrote something his mum could read back to him.

- Ivan recognised the number 3 today for the first time.
- Sammy said, 'The numbers on this side of the road go up in twos'.
- Akina cut her piece of paper into two pieces and said, 'Half each'.

## What to do with your observations

The first and most obvious thing you do with your observations is use them to plan what to offer next. In this way you are basing your planned programme on the interests and needs of the children as you have observed them. So observation informs planning. You will remember how we talked in the last chapter about how planning based on the observed interests and needs of individual children ensures that the programme provided offers genuine equality of access and opportunity to all children. So you are using your observations to identify what each child knows and can do so that you can plan what you need to offer to take each child's learning forward. From your observations you will set about planning activities that are relevant and motivating for the children.

Once you have used your observations to plan what to offer next you can also think about how to use them to build a record of the child's progress over time. Inevitably, if all members of staff are keeping notes on what they notice, you will gather a veritable mountain of paper over the days and weeks. It is here that you need to use your judgement about what is significant. I would suggest that each keyworker be responsible for collecting together the bits of paper relating to her key children. She then needs to sift through them, extracting what is significant and discarding the rest. There is absolutely no point in keeping every observation note made. What you want to do is track each child's progress and the best way of doing this is to chart the leaps in learning mentioned earlier in this chapter.

You will want to ensure that you have observation notes covering all aspects of the curriculum. Where you have been worried about a child's emotional development it is natural that your observation notes will reflect this. But the child's overall development needs to be charted and you need to ensure that you have noticed something about the child's learning across the six areas of learning.

## Interpreting what you see

Writing down what you see and hear is easy enough. It is like taking a photograph or making a tape-recording. You record exactly what happens. But, as we have said earlier, observations on their own are of little use. What you need to do is interpret what you see and hear to understand what it shows you about the child's learning and development.

Let us look at some examples:

Four-year-old Abdul has recently arrived in the country from Bangladesh and does not yet have any English. You notice that he likes to go into the book corner and sort out all the books according to size.

*What does this tell you about his current interests? What does it suggest that he is paying attention to? And what might you introduce next to take this interest forward?*
Do you think he might be interested in size? Or perhaps in sorting things out? Did you think about bringing in some boxes of different sizes, inviting him to sort the books, by size, into the boxes? Did you think of reading the story – and using props to make it come alive for Abdul – of *Goldilocks and the Three Bears*? Did you think about introducing objects of varying sizes in the home corner as a follow-up to this – three different sized beds, three different sized teddies, three different sized bowls and so on?

Four-year-old Amy loves books. She knows many of the books in the playgroup by heart and often chooses to look at books. One day you notice that she is actually drawing her finger under the text as she reads and that her retelling of the story is very close to the text.

*What do you think she already knows? What do you think she is paying attention to? If you feel she is paying attention to print, what might you plan next to help her take the next step?*
Drummond cites the example of a four-year-old girl who examines shells and pebbles under several different types of magnifiers. She spends a long time bringing the lens close to her eye and then moving it away again. She then picks up a shell, examines it under the magnifier on a tripod and then holds it to each ear in turn. Then she puts the shell again under the tripod, but this time places her ear, rather than her eye, against the magnifying glass as though she were trying to magnify the sound. Drummond asks:

Whatever was she doing? Was she ignorant? Or stupid? No, neither of these. As I watched I realised she was asking a question, not out loud, but privately, to herself. She had established that the magnifying glass made the shell look bigger, now she wanted to know 'will it make it louder?'

(Drummond 1998, p. 102)

Close observation allows us to make guesses about what children already know and about what their current interests are. But, since we make our guesses in light of what we already know about that particular child, and also what we know about how young children learn, these are educated guesses. So we use what we see and hear (our observation notes) as the information or evidence we gather and then interpret this in light of our knowledge to help us plan what we will offer next to take learning forward.

## Building up a profile

One of the best ways of keeping track of children's progress is to start a profile for each child. This can be in the form of a file or notebook for each child and in this profile you can place some vital information.

Profiling can be defined as the process of assessing, recording and gathering evidence of children's progress and achievement over time. This ongoing process of evaluating progress is what is called 'formative assessment', and ideally a profile should include information gathered about the child from the child him- or herself (where possible), from the parents and from all the practitioners involved with the child.

A profile might include the following:

- some examples or samples of children's work;
- some comments written by practitioners about children's progress;
- some attempt by practitioners to analyse children's work and progress;
- comments from parents about the child's interests at home and about the child's progress in the setting;
- any comments the child might have made which show evidence of the child reflecting on his or her learning.

To illustrate this, here is an extract from the profile for four-year-old Farida:

a) samples of work plus comments of adults

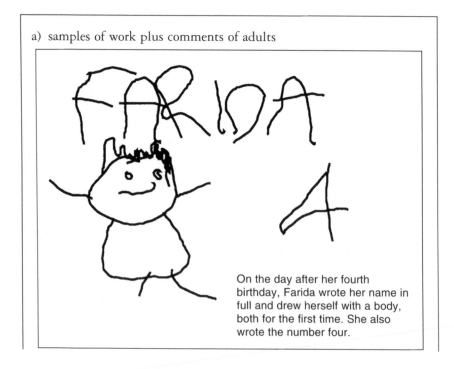

On the day after her fourth birthday, Farida wrote her name in full and drew herself with a body, both for the first time. She also wrote the number four.

b) examples of workers' analysis of learning

29/4/96: Farida has come on in leaps and bounds. She spends a lot of time in the book corner and knows many of the books by heart. She can now retell a story, and turns the pages, using the pictures to help her. She is writing her name and is just starting to talk about letters. She spends a lot of time painting, drawing and making things. In the workshop area this week she made a box for her mother – choosing materials carefully and then decorated it with elaborate patterns of objects stuck to the surface.

c) parent's comments

I am happy with how Farida is getting on. She likes the playgroup and is looking forward to going to school. At home she looks at books a lot and sings lots of songs. She also likes to write.

d) child's comments

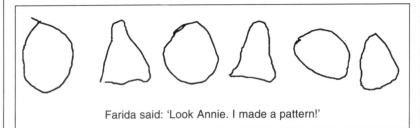

Farida said: 'Look Annie. I made a pattern!'

'Look, Annie. I made a pattern': Farida knew what a pattern was.
'Annie, I can write my name and my brother's name now. It goes F A R O U K – like this!': Farida knows what she can write and is proud of her achievements.

Profiling is time-consuming, but you can see that a real picture of the child emerges from this. If you think about how much information a parent or teacher can get from such a profile you will realise that the amount of work is justified. But a word of warning! Please limit the amount of information you put into the profile. You need to learn to be selective and only include things that add to what you already know about the child. Don't, for example, include two samples of writing unless the second shows some way in which the child's writing has developed. And do remember to date all samples and comments and always to say why something has been included.

## Involving parents

It is a cliché to say that parents know more about their own child than anyone else, but like most clichés it is true. Practitioners and teachers do, of course, get to know children well, but it is important to recognise that their knowledge of the child is limited. The person who sees the child in every situation at every time of the day and year is the parent. Parents are, indeed, experts when it comes to their own child. Despite this fact, many parents are made to feel that they know nothing and that their understanding of the child may be flawed or limited. This applies particularly to parents whose first language is not English or to parents who feel threatened by the education system and by authority. These parents find it difficult to have their voices heard and tend to adopt the stance that 'Teacher and playgroup practitioners know best!'

All parents, whatever their culture, language, background, social class or gender, care about their children. Parents who send young children to a nursery or crèche or playgroup do so for many reasons: some because they feel their children will benefit from contact with other children; some because they want their children to have a head start in the education stakes; some because they need or want to work or study. But all parents want the best for their children and all parents deserve to be kept informed about how their children are making progress.

In the Italian nurseries, described in an earlier chapter, a great deal of work goes into keeping parents informed about their children's progress. Each child has a plastic wallet up on the wall and staff put into these brief comments about what the child has done that day. For parents of very young children, this information makes them feel involved in their children's progress. No parent wants to miss their own child's first step or first word. Parents of older children are equally entitled to learn of their children's progress. What is more, they will notice changes in their child's behaviour and learning at home and can add these to the child's profile.

Involving parents in this process is sometimes difficult and always requires that practitioners be sensitive and supportive in their approach. Most nurseries and playgroups collect information from parents when the child starts in the nursery. This will often include practical details, but some nurseries now invite parents to say something about their child's interests, fears, passions, likes and dislikes. This gives practitioners some starting point on which to base their assessment of progress. After all, all children starting in the nursery or playgroup come with a history. No child arrives as a blank slate. You can only assess progress against some starting point.

This involvement of parents is a good starting point, but a partnership with parents needs to go further than this. Many nurseries and playgroups now invite parents to become involved in contributing to the child's profile. Parents are invited to read through the profile and add their comments.

You will, of course, need to think carefully about how you can manage this process in a way that allows those parents who have English as an additional language to have equal access to the partnership.

## Summative assessment

The type of assessment we have been looking at is known as formative assessment. It is what you do all the time in your work both in order to ensure that the children are making progress and that what you are offering is providing the necessary challenge and support to ensure that this happens. Formative assessment is crucial to any educational enterprise.

Summative assessment is the type of assessment that summarises a child's achievements at a particular point in time. The most obvious example of summative assessment is the end-of-year report. You will remember from your own school days how getting the school report could either be an occasion for celebration or one for misery. School reports used to consist, often, of a mark or grade accompanied by a very brief and bald comment – something like 'Judy has done very well at PE this term' or 'Marcus needs to try harder'. These comments gave parents no indication of exactly what the child had achieved over the year. Nor did it give any indication of what particular problems might be – nor any recommended course of action.

Nowadays summative assessments are better in that they do try and summarise all that practitioners or teachers have found from their formative assessments over a period of time. If you look back to the profiles, you can see how the practitioner could, at the end of a term or a year, make some comments summarising the child's progress in all areas of learning. Practitioners should examine the early learning goals which will give them a framework against which they can make summative statements.

Here is an example:

> *Personal, social and emotional development*: Farida started the year very timidly. She tended to play alone and was often observed to be rather withdrawn. Over the year, as her self-esteem and ability to use English have developed, so has her confidence. As she moves into the reception class she has already met a number of the early learning goals. She is interested and motivated to learn and confident to try new activities. She can concentrate for long periods of time and has formed good relationships with both adults and other children. She understands a lot about right and wrong and is very independent. She likes to work as part of a group and has developed a particular friendship with Harinder.
>
> *Communication, language and literacy*: Farida has made great strides in this learning area and again already meets several of the early learning goals.

She listens with enjoyment to songs and rhymes and knows many by heart. She can retell some stories and her favourites are 'Peepo' and 'Brown Bear'. She can recognise her own name and those of her friends and knows that, in English, print is read from left to right and top to bottom. She enjoys making up stories and knows the difference between writing and drawing. She often chooses to write letters, books, cards or to fill in blank forms. She can write her own name and those of her brother and sister.

*Mathematical development*: Farida counts reliably to 12 and recognises the symbols to 10. She enjoys making patterns in her drawing and in her play with blocks and also enjoys exploring space. She uses the language of mathematics very well (high, low, underneath, heavy, etc.) She uses her developing mathematical ideas to solve practical problems that she encounters in her play.

*Creative development*: Farida enjoys choosing materials and tools to make things. She likes exploring colour and shape and enjoys painting, using clay and making things in the workshop area. She explores colour, texture and shape in both two and three dimensions. She enjoys singing and dancing and spends much of her time in complex role play both inside and out. She likes to play the musical instruments.

*Physical development*: Farida has overcome her initial nervousness and now enjoys playing outdoors and in, moving with confidence and imagination, with increased control and coordination. She can run, jump, balance, catch and throw. She uses a wide range of tools with great skill and manages fine tools like pens and pencils effectively.

*Knowledge and understanding of the world*: Farida is curious and interested in many things. She often asks questions and enjoys investigating objects and materials using all her senses. She talks about patterns and differences and similarities. She often tries things out and discusses what is happening. She is willing to take risks. She knows a great deal about her own language and culture and shares with adults and children with whom she feels comfortable.

Farida has made great strides and has been a delightful member of the nursery community. She will enjoy learning in the same way in the reception class.

You can see how a summative record like this gives some picture of the child's development in all the areas of learning over a period of time. A record like this sent to the receiving teacher will give her or him some indication of what the child has already done and what the child's interests and strengths are. A teacher receiving Farida's report would be unlikely to assume that Farida knows nothing about reading and writing, for example. There is clear evidence of what she already knows and this provides the teacher with some indication of where to start her or his programme for this child.

## Summing it up

Everyone involved in the education and care of young children has a professional obligation to document children's progress. This is a difficult task and one that many practitioners find daunting. It is important to remember that your setting needs to work out a policy on how this is to be done.

- The only way you can know how children are progressing is to observe them as they play and to write down your observations.
- Everyone involved with the child should contribute to this.
- The observation notes on their own are only of use if you analyse them to find what they show you about what the child already knows and can do, what the child is interested in and/or paying attention to.
- On the basis of this you can evaluate both the child's progress and how well you are meeting the child's needs.
- Observation then suggests what you should plan next in order that children can take the next step in their learning.
- Parents and children should be involved in the assessment process.
- One way of doing this is to build up profiles for each child in which practitioners carefully select examples of children's work (and these can include photographs of things the child has done), their own comments and evaluations, comments from children and from parents.
- Even very young children can contribute to their profiles. What you are looking for are examples of children reflecting on what they can do or what they have achieved.
- Parents are experts about their own children: their views on children's progress are essential.
- Parents should be invited, on entering the setting, to give information that includes details of the child's interests and experiences. This provides a baseline against which progress can be assessed.
- All parents need to be involved in this partnership and ways need to be found of involving those parents who, for one reason or another, may be reluctant or unable to contribute.
- A good programme of formative assessment can lead to summative assessment which carries information that is meaningful to parents and of use to receiving teachers or practitioners.
- It is time-consuming and difficult, but worth the effort!

# References

Ackers, J. (1994) '"Why Involve Me?" Encouraging Children and their Parents to Participate in the Assessment Process', in L. Abbott and R. Rodger (eds), *Quality Education in the Early Years*, Buckingham, Open University Press.

Bartholomew, L. and Bruce, T. (1994) *Getting to Know You: A Guide to Record Keeping in Early Childhood Education and Care*, London, Hodder and Stoughton.

Devereux, J. (1996) 'What We See Depends on What We Look For: Observation as Part of Teaching and Learning in the Early Years', in S. Robson and S. Smedley (eds), *Education in Early Childhood*, London, David Fulton.

DfEE and QCA (2000) *Curriculum Guidance for the Foundation Stage*, London, DfEE.

Drummond, M.J. (1994) *Assessing Children's Learning*, London, David Fulton.

Drummond, M.J. (1998) 'Observing Children', in S. Smidt (ed.), *The Early Years: A Reader*, London, Routledge.

# Chapter 9

# Partnerships with parents

The *Curriculum Guidance for the Foundation Stage* reminds all of us involved in the care and education of young children of the importance of working closely with parents. Parents we all know and appreciate are children's first educators. They teach children (without giving them lessons, having learning objectives or a system of stars and smiley faces) to talk, to walk, to dress themselves, to know who they are in the world and to express their ideas and emotions. There is a wealth of documented evidence showing that where parents and practitioners work closely together children thrive. It is imperative that in any setting a genuine two-way partnership is established. This means that information goes from setting to home and from home to setting. It means that any setting spends time establishing some ground rules about how to set up such a partnership in order that the following principles are followed:

- practitioners show respect for and understanding of the particular role of each parents as primary educator;
- practitioners talk to parents about their expectations of the setting and explain to parents the curriculum, the routines, the ethos and the philosophy;
- practitioners talk to parents about their child – about his or her development and about any concerns they may have;
- settling-in arrangements are thoughtful and allow time for children to be secure;
- all parents are made welcome and can see evidence of their culture and languages in the setting;
- the particular knowledge, skills and expertise of parents is used to support the learning activities on offer;
- parents are kept informed about what is happening on a daily, weekly and longer-term basis;
- parents are kept informed about what the children are doing and learning;
- parents have the opportunity to contribute to assessments made of their own children (to records and profiles);

- parents are invited to read with children and play games with them at home so that the divisions between home and school are minimised.

You may be interested in this. It is the account of how seven-month-old Sam was inducted into his nursery which is part of the fantastic early years provision in Reggio Emilia in Italy.

His mother, Jenny Leask, tells us that their first meeting was with the two full-time teachers who would be with him, together with the school cook, who was regarded as a key figure in the school. The parents were asked detailed questions about Sam as a little boy. What did he like doing? How did he like to be held? How did he behave when he was tired? The answers they gave were written down and when Sam started, three weeks later, his parents found this little biography of their son and his photograph displayed on the wall alongside similar little histories of the other new children. Displayed too were details of the parents: names, dates of birth, professions, etc. – 'it dawned on us that we were part of that group too, about to become part of the school'.

If you want to know more about the care paid to settling-in procedures and parental partnerships do read Leask's article in *Experiencing Reggio Emilia* (Abbott and Nutbrown 2001).

## Parents and schools: a potted history

The role of parents with regard to the education of their children out of the home has a long and difficult history. There were those who held that teachers were professionals who knew best about what young children needed and that parents should be happy to hand over their young children without question into such capable hands. Home and school were kept separate with no recognition of the fact that learning begins at home and that parents are fundamentally involved in the education process.

When the importance of the role of parents began to be recognised it was in the sense that 'good' parents are able to help their children's learning by supporting what happens in the school or nursery. 'Bad' parents were seen to hold children back. For several decades it was believed that it was the role of schools and teachers to educate these 'inadequate' parents (who were invariably poor or black) and to compensate for the perceived inadequacies of the home. This view was exemplified in programmes like 'The Head Start' programme in the USA. Even the Plowden Report in 1967, which advocated partnership with parents, saw the role of parents limited to that of raising funds and being informed about their children's progress and development by teachers through regular meetings. So parents continued to play a largely passive role – receiving information rather than contributing to children's progress. It is only in recent years that a different view of parents has emerged, and much of that has to do with the work of researchers like Tizard and Hughes (1984) and Gordon Wells (1986) who demonstrated effectively that most homes, regardless of socio-economic level or other factors, provide rich learning environments. Alongside this has come a recognition that parents know more about their own children than teachers and playgroup workers do and if children are to be offered rich learning experiences in the nursery and playgroup which allow them to build on what they already know, this expertise of parents needs to be made accessible to all those working with the child.

The changing role of parents is reflected at the official level. Under the 1944 Education Act parents were seen as having a duty to ensure that their children received education suitable to their age and ability. The Taylor Report (1977) emphasised parental responsibility, but did recognise that individual parents might need to band together in order to have a collective voice. The report advocated that parents should have equal representation with teachers, the local education authority and the local community on school governing bodies. The 1980 Education Act, which followed this report, only partly implemented these recommendations and it was only with the 1986 Education (No. 2) Act that parents were given equal representation with local education authority members. The Act further required that all schools furnish parents with an annual report and hold an annual meeting for parents.

The most important piece of legislation recognising that parents have rights as well as responsibilities came in the early 1980s with the Warnock Report which looked at children with special needs. In this report teachers and schools were required to seek the full involvement of parents and the notion of parental/school partnerships really emerged.

In the late 1980s with the publication of the 1988 Education Act the role of parents shifted again, with the emphasis now being placed on parental choice. This notion of parental choice is a key theme underpinning much of current government legislation – as you will realise when you consider relatively recent legislation regarding nursery education. It is exemplified in the Parents Charter (1994). This document suggests that parents can influence schools significantly through their right to choose schools for their children. It also suggests that parents become 'active partners with the school and its teachers'. This approach shifts education to a new arena – that of the market-place – and places responsibilities on parents to exercise their rights as consumers.

*You might like to consider this in depth and decide whether you feel that education is best situated in the market-place and whether the concept of parents as consumers is the best way forward in establishing good relationships.*

You can see from this how parents, over the past twenty years, have been given some rights individually to be involved with the education of their children and some collective rights in terms of serving on governing bodies, which now have increased powers.

## Why involve parents?

Nowadays it is rare to find anybody who doesn't think that parental involvement in education is a 'good' thing. But defining quite why this is so is complex. Here are some suggestions, drawn from Robson (1996).

*Parents have rights and schools and settings need to be accountable to parents.* The Children Act (1989) states that all parents have responsibilities towards their own children and these include concern for their care and education. More importantly, however, is the fact that parents are their child's first educators and have a continuing concern for their child's education away from the home. This view enshrines the rights of all parents to be consulted and informed about their child's progress and makes institutions involved in the care and education of children accountable to parents.

*Parents can have a positive effect on their children's attainment and progress.* Tizard *et al.* (1988) showed that 97 per cent of parents of children in the reception class helped them at home with reading. They had similar findings with regard to parents helping their children with mathematics. A number of schemes for involving parents more directly with their children's work in schools have revealed gains. Working-class parents are as keen and able to help their children with learning at home as more middle-class parents. The fact that all parents want their children to do well at nursery and school has important implications for how workers relate to parents.

*Parental involvement in the school can help minimise conflicts between the values of home and school.* We have touched on this in earlier chapters. Since all schools and settings serve diverse communities with different value systems the more that is known about these values and beliefs the better the relationship between parents and workers. Where workers are able to understand and consider different styles and expectations they are more likely to be able to arrive at a shared and common way of approaching both care and education.

*Parental involvement in the school can have positive spin-off effects for parents themselves.* Where parents are invited to become actively involved in the life of the nursery they gain insights into what it is the workers are doing and why. So where a school or setting takes time and trouble to explain to parents the reasons for providing play opportunities or why reading to children is important, for example, parents themselves learn and may be able to implement some of what they have learned at home.

*Parental involvement in the school can have positive spin-off effects for teachers and workers.* Where parents are actively involved in the nursery, workers have the opportunity to learn more about the parent and child, about the values and principles operating within the child's life out of the setting. Since one of the underpinning principles of high-quality early learning is building on what children already know and can do, the more that is known about the child's life in all its aspects the better the provision within the nursery or setting is likely to be.

*Parents can offer workers and teachers support.* Where partnerships with parents are established the support of parents can be a powerful tool when change and improvement is sought. There are many examples of parents taking action in order to ensure that a playgroup acquires better premises or in supporting workers' requests for better pay and conditions.

## The implications of this for settings

It is clear from this that establishing a close and respectful attitude between parents and workers is crucial to the well-being of the children. Research shows that all parents, regardless of class or cultural group or social position, want what is best for their children. All parents are keen to help their children and many will give up a great deal to see their children succeed.

One of the difficulties, however, is that there are parents who do not know the best way in which to do this and who lack the confidence to approach staff. There are also many parents who have a limited command of English and who are often dependent on getting a second-hand version through translation. These may be very real barriers to establishing partnerships and are issues that are certainly worth addressing.

Another very real barrier may be the attitude of staff to parents. Where parents are perceived as being 'too pushy' or 'not interested', establishing relationships can be difficult. It is worthwhile examining your own attitudes to the parents of the children in your setting and seeing if you can honestly define parents who make you uncomfortable for one reason or another.

*Try to work out what it is that makes you uncomfortable and think of ways in which you can overcome your prejudice.*

Here is what Martha, a worker at a playgroup said:

> I realised that Tommy's mother made me feel very uncomfortable. She is a teacher and very confident. Every day she would come in and ask what Tommy had done that day. I always felt that she was critical, although she never actually said anything critical. I used to dread open evenings. Then the organiser of the playgroup suggested that we had some social occasions for parents where we invited a small group of parents in to talk about their expectations for their children. We tried to plan groups that were very mixed, and in the group with Tommy's mother was a mother who speaks Turkish, a single parent and a very young mother. I started by telling them what we were planning and what our aims were and then asked for their comments. I was really surprised when Tommy's mother said that she was hoping that Tommy would develop his self-confidence and his independence and his ability to get on with children of his own age. She said she was very happy with his progress at the playgroup and she reassured the very young mother, whose child had only just joined. And she was really nice to the Turkish

mother and showed her pictures of what the children had been doing. I had to revise my opinion of her!

## How to involve parents as equal partners

We may not all manage to do as much as the settings in Reggio Emilia, but there are many things we already do and many things we might consider doing to help build genuine partnerships

### Home visiting

It is recognised that moving away from home for the first time is traumatic for both child and parent. Many schools and nurseries try to reduce the level of stress by visiting the child and parent at home before the child actually starts in the setting. The obvious advantage of this is that the initial contact takes place in a situation which is familiar and where the parent is in control. But this is a sensitive area and there may well be parents who do not want to be visited at home – particularly where the parent is living in temporary accommodation or where the parent sees the visit as a way of outsiders assessing the 'quality' of the home and of the parents. The rights of parents to refuse a visit should be respected and it is important that the school or setting is clear about the purpose of the visit and able to explain this to parents.

Here is how one nursery teacher sees the purpose of home visits:

> It is our policy that each child gets this opportunity to meet me in the safety of her/his home environment . . . I usually take a puzzle, a book, some drawing material and a photo book with pictures of the team, the school, our class, and the children at work. We look through this book together, often with grandparents, aunts and uncles, as well as parents and the child and siblings. I chat a bit about the kinds of things children can do in our class. The pictures speak for themselves when I am unable to communicate in the family's language. That, and a great deal of body language, smiles, gestures usually gets the message across.
>
> During the visit I also take some photographs of the child. They are used later when the child comes to school to make her/his space on the coat hooks, the towel hook and the third, a whole-body one, for the magnet board. The home visit is a good opportunity to ask the parents to write their child's name in the family's language . . . From there I can enlarge it on the photocopier at school and use it in our graphics area and anywhere else where the child's name appears in English.
>
> (Voss 1998, p. 47)

### Visiting the nursery or setting

All children and their parents should visit the setting prior to the child starting. You may want to think about sending an individual invitation to the child and parent, making the visit something special. Many settings find that allowing parents and children to visit as often as possible eases the child's entry to the setting and makes the parent feel more comfortable. It is important to try to ensure that not too many new children and parents visit at one time. The best way of making parents and children feel important and valued is to allow one member of staff (perhaps the keyworker) time to be able to talk to both parent and child. It is worth considering the point that these initial visits are going to be the time when the parent or carer forms her or his initial impression of the setting, so it is important that they are carefully planned for.

### Settling in

Some children find the transition from visiting to attending the setting on a permanent basis easy; others – as you will well know – find it difficult. The child's distress will convey itself to the parent and this may damage the relationship with the setting. You will want to consider your settling-in arrangements with care. Most settings invite (indeed often insist) that parents stay with children at least for the first few days. You will want to think about how you handle this with parents who cannot manage because of work or domestic commitments. The presence of parent or carer is reassuring for the child and if you want parents or carers to be able to stay with the child you need to give them adequate notice of this. Most settings also advise parents to tell children when they are leaving and not just to disappear.

### Staying in touch

Parents, leaving young children in the care of others, feel that they are missing out on significant moments in their child's development. You will have read in an earlier chapter how the nurseries in Reggio Emilia keep parents in touch with what their children have done each day. There are many different ways of doing this – from wall displays to link books that go between home and setting to informal chats at the start or the end of the day. In addition to this you will want to ensure that you arrange particular times when parents can come in and have an in-depth discussion about their child's progress. Do remember that the timing of this is important. If you have evening meetings there may be parents who will not attend. Similarly meetings during the day will exclude some parents. You need to work with parents to find out which is the best time for them and to do your best to meet this.

### Involving parents in assessing progress

Parents need and should be involved in both commenting on what they observe about their child's progress and development at home and contributing to what workers observe about development within the setting. If you operate a profile system in your setting you will ensure that parents' voices are heard.

### Involving parents in the day-to-day life of the setting

Many nurseries and playgroups invite parents in to help during the day. This help may vary from reading to children to cooking with them or accompanying them on outings and so on. However parents are involved, it is important that their role is clearly spelled out to them so that they know what it is they are doing and why. This implies that workers will have to talk to parents about what they are doing and why. This is one of the best ways of genuinely involving parents in the life of the nursery. You may invite a parent in for a specific purpose: perhaps a mother who has just had a new baby or a father who is a nurse. Again, an explanation of what you want them to do on this visit is important.

### Home/school projects

Many settings try to find ways of offering parents things to do at home to build on what has happened in the nursery or setting during the week. Parents may be invited to take home books to read with children or to borrow toys from a toy library. An initial meeting with new parents to introduce the materials and explain ways in which they may be used is useful for parents who may feel reluctant to do things that they see as 'not their role'.

### Offering learning opportunities to parents

Some nurseries place great emphasis on their role in educating parents. Some are able to offer parents classes ranging from what to do about temper tantrums or bed-wetting to classes in English as an additional language. This is, of course, very dependent on your resources, but if you have a spare room in your setting you might want to consider offering such classes.

## Summing it up

A great deal has been written about the importance of partnerships with parents and you can find some of the books and chapters in the list at the end of this chapter. Partnership with parents is fundamental to a successful learning environment for all children, but particularly for children in their first steps away from home.

- All parents want the very best for their children.
- All parents are crucial in the education and development of their own children.
- A partnership with parents, based on mutual respect, will benefit everyone concerned.
- Parents need to be made to feel that they are worth listening and talking to.
- Settings need to ensure that the environment is welcoming to all parents and that all parents know that successful education is a joint enterprise.
- The ways in which parents can become involved need to be clear and explicit.
- Parents' fears need to be acknowledged.
- Workers need to ensure that they are willing to give information, but equally willing to receive it.
- Settling-in procedures need to be carefully considered and explained to parents.
- Settings need to decide how they will ensure that parents with little or no English are not disadvantaged.
- Sometimes having a theme based on the observed interests of the children allows settings to establish strong partnerships with parents, particularly where the theme selected provides opportunities for parents to contribute their own skills, their knowledge, their talents and their experience.

## References

Abbott, L. and Nutbrown, C. (eds) (2001) *Experiencing Reggio Emilia: Implications for Pre-School Provision*, Oxford, Oxford University Press.

DfEE and QCA (2000) *Curriculum Guidance for the Foundation Stage*, London, DfEE.

Hannon, P. and Weinberger, I. (1994) 'Sharing Ideas about Pre-School Literacy with Parents', in H. Dombey and M. Meek (eds), *First Steps Together: Home–School Early Literacy in European Contexts*, Stoke on Trent, Trentham Books.

Hannon, P., Weinberger, J. and Nutbrown, C. (1991) 'A Study of Work with Parents to Promote Early Literacy Development', *Research Papers in Education*, 6(2).

Leask, J. (2001) 'Sam's Invisible Extra Gear – A Parent's View', in L. Abbott and C. Nutbrown (eds), *Experiencing Reggio Emilia: Implications for Pre-School Provision*, Oxford, Oxford University Press.

Robson, S. (1996) 'Home and School: A Potentially Powerful Partnership', in S. Robson and S. Smedley (eds), *Education in Early Childhood*, London, David Fulton.

Tizard, B. and Hughes, M. (1984) *Young Children Learning*, London, Fontana.

Tizard, B., Blatchford, B., Burke, J., Farquar, C. and Lewis, I. (1988) *Young Children at School in the Inner City*, London, Lawrence Erlbaum.

Voss, B. (1998) 'Supporting Young Children', in S. Smidt (ed.), *The Early Years: A Reader*, London, Routledge.

Wells, G. (1986) *The Meaning Makers*, London, Hodder and Stoughton.

# Index